A VOICE FOR THE MUTE SWAN

A VOICE
FOR THE
MUTE
SWAN

WRITTEN AND ILLUSTRATED BY

Gail A. Glaser, VN

WITH A FOREWORD BY
JEREMY HANLEY, MP

WHITTET BOOKS

First published 1989
Text and illustrations © 1989 by Gail Glaser
Whittet Books, 18 Anley Road, London W14 0BY

Design by Paul Minns

The author and publishers gratefully acknowledge the permission
of the following to reproduce colour photographs between the following
pages: pp. 48/9 Eckart Pott/Bruce Coleman, Hans Reinhard/Bruce Coleman,
Jane Burton/Bruce Coleman and Peter Laub/Ardea, pp. 64/5 Wardene Weisser/Ardea,
George Rapkins; pp. 96/7 Richard Vaughan/Ardea, S. Nielsen/Bruce Coleman.

British Library Cataloguing in Publication Data
Glaser, Gail A.
  A voice for the mute swan.
  1. Mute Swan
  I. Title
  598.4'1

ISBN 0-905483-73-1

Printed and bound by Bath Press, Bath

Contents

Acknowledgments

Particular thanks to veterinary surgeon Steve Cooke and his wife Zyllah from whom I have learnt so much; to Dr Mike Birkhead who years ago answered many beginner's tedious questions and showed me post-mortems; to Dr Jane Sears for her help and advice to date; to Bill Colley, swan-marker to the Worshipful Company of Vintners also for help and advice in those very busy years; to veterinary surgeon Mike Winch who unwittingly began my work with swans; to all my long-suffering friends and colleagues at the RSPCA, particularly Inspector Andy Foxcroft and Inspector Bill Alston; and to Jeremy Hanley MP for much personal support on behalf of the swans and for his invaluable debate in the House of Commons.

Foreword

There are many birds that have come to be associated with nations, but none symbolizes the tranquillity of warm summer days beside the meandering rivers of England quite like our swan. Their grace and beauty are an irreplaceable feature of rivers such as the Thames and the Stratford Avon as well as the Norfolk Broads. It was noticed, however, during the 1970s that flocks of swans in many parts of the country were diminishing, and by 1978 the swans upon the Avon at Stratford had all but disappeared. On the Thames the numbers declined dramatically, as during the 1956 annual swan-upping there were found to be 1311 swans and cygnets on the Thames, but in 1982 between Putney and Henley the number had dropped to 255. In July 1988 during swan-upping a total of 340 birds were sighted as opposed to 250 birds the previous year. This total included breeding pairs of swans, cygnets and non-breeding juvenile swans.

In 1983 of the 19 swans that underwent a post mortem, from the Kingston to Richmond stretch, 17 died as a direct result of lead poisoning, although the Edward Grey Institute in its research has discovered that whilst poisoning from anglers' lead weights is the most common cause of death, fishing tackle, power cables, disease, archery and shooting all have their place in swan mortality.

I raised the subject in a debate in the House of Commons on the 18th January, 1984 and in response the Under Secretary of State for the Environment, the Hon William Waldegrave, MP, promised the House that if anglers were not prepared voluntarily to switch to non-toxic alternatives during the next three years to the 1st January, 1987, he would not hesitate to legislate. Whilst there was tremendous cooperation by official angling bodies, aided by professional anglers, the angling press and the manufacturers of weights, old habits died very hard indeed. True to his word, Mr Waldegrave issued a ban on the lead weights that were causing such damage at the beginning of 1987. Potentially, a great victory for the mute swan, but anglers still continued to ignore the ban, and in 1987 60% of all swan deaths on our rivers were caused by ingestion of lead.

Gail Glaser makes a plea for these lovely birds and their protection, describing their sufferings and the work of treating them with a dedication and love that is an inspiration to read. If this book makes further progress in arresting needless and cruel deaths for one of the most beautiful birds in the world, then she and thousands with her will be happy.

Jeremy Hanley
House of Commons, 1988

Introduction

My early aspirations of a career involving animals, and in particular wildlife, were frustrated when I developed various allergies. However, after four years at art college and five years working in television I was still not reconciled to abandoning that ambition. By chance I met Mike Tomkies, a wildlife photographer/writer, who, having overcome considerable setbacks himself, simply suggested that if this area was where my heart really lay then I would find a way of getting there. Spurred on by this advice, and several other timely incidents, I set about remedying the situation. The finding of a severely injured cat near the M1 motorway one dark winter morning led me to the doors of the RSPCA and by the time my journey back to the country was completed my decision was made. With the help of a very understanding doctor I began a long course of desensitizing injections and in 1979, one and a half years later, I was working with the RSPCA at their hospital in Putney, South London. The RSPCA not only gave me a training as a veterinary nurse but, most importantly, provided me with the opportunity to do a vast amount of practical nursing and I was able to care for a wide variety of wildlife.

The Mute Swan, as have many other species, has suffered from man's encroachment into the places where it lives. In my early days with the RSPCA I began to see more and more swans brought in for veterinary treatment with varying problems; as time passed the instances of birds coming in with complicated problems such as lead poisoning increased considerably. Very little seemed known about the swan as a species in terms of its specialized treatment and care. At this time I was introduced to veterinary surgeon Steve Cooke.

Based near Windsor in Berkshire, Steve Cooke and his wife Zyllah had already been working desperately hard for some years on the diverse veterinary and welfare needs of the Mute Swan. They had in fact formed a charity, 'Save Our Swans', to rescue, treat and rehabilitate sick and injured swans. Steve had also pioneered a very successful programme of treatment for lead poisoning in swans. From then on it was to them that I referred whenever necessary. This was, needless to say, almost all of the time. Their practical advice and help was always available, and the more I knew about swans, the more I realized how much specialist care they needed. I made many hasty journeys down the M4 motorway to Windsor; with the swan or swans comfortably restrained for the journey, it was usually fellow motorists who were more surprised by these events than the swans themselves, though all too often I had a creature on board which was too sick to care what was happening.

To treat swans successfully one must have considerable understanding not only of their illnesses and how to treat them medically, but also their behaviour, motivations and needs in the wild. Each swan is an individual. They have markedly different characters and may react totally differently to the same situation; they have various levels of tolerance in potentially stressful conditions. Swans are highly intelligent creatures. This becomes clear the more one studies them and in the case of birds in care, diligent observation is invaluable to all concerned.

To this day the study, rescue and treatment of the Mute Swan population continues, though I am less directly involved. Despite some beneficial changes and the encouraging decrease in overall swan mortality there is still some way to go before we can cease to be concerned for the fate of the Mute Swan. Throughout the country people continue to care for swans, including the RSPCA, Len Baker's 'Swan Rescue Europe' based in Norfolk and Dot Beeson and her family who take in swans at their Swan Sanctuary in Egham, Surrey. I first met Tim Heron when I joined 'Save Our Swans' as a committee member. Tim had worked for many years helping swans and was an indispensable part of the charity. When 'Save Our Swans' had to close Tim formed a new charity 'Swan Lifeline', now a registered charity. Steve and Zyllah Cooke are still engaged in research and continue to advise Swan Lifeline and other charities. Margerie Unwin, 'Swan Lifeline'(Outwood), in Surrey also takes swans in on behalf of the charity (see p.123 for contact numbers).

Considering the size of the Mute Swan and its special needs, we believe it is still an urgent priority to establish, in the South of England, a proper fully equipped hospital with sufficient land

and aquatic facilities to cope perfectly with the many swans that need to be cared for.

I have written this book because I felt the need to express affection and concern for a beautiful species which has had to endure so much needless suffering. I have attempted to write only about the things that I have learnt during my work and from my own personal encounters with swans. Detailed information on the biology of swans may be found in more academic works. I have limited myself to writing about my own experiences.

Caring for swans is a bitter-sweet experience. I have seen many swans and cygnets die. The sadness, and certainly anger, one feels when they become needlessly sick or injured and die is matched only by the exhilaration one feels on seeing other swans regain their natural grace and beauty.

I became especially involved with particular swans and can honestly say that they changed the course of my life. Despite everything that could be done for them, some of them died. It is my greatest hope that, with thousands of other swans and cygnets, their deaths will ultimately not have been in vain. On their behalf and to the best of my ability, this book is a Voice for the Mute Swan.

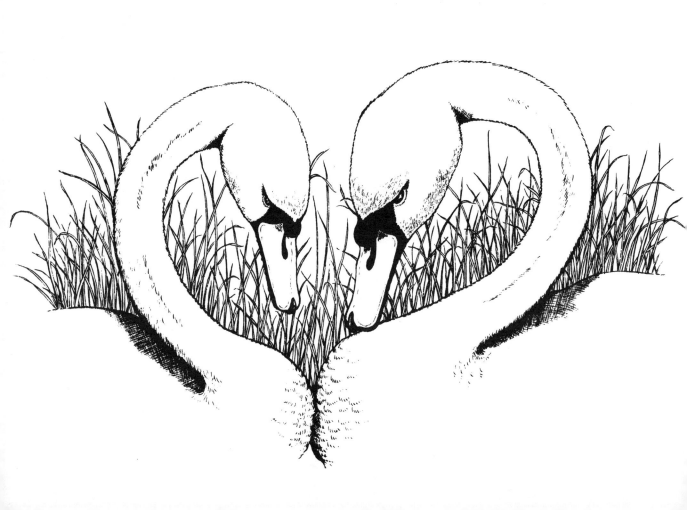

1 The Life Cycle of the Mute Swan

Mute Swans prefer to live in areas of slow-flowing water with plenty of vegetation, so smaller rivers and their backwaters are ideal. They are quite adaptable so will commonly be found on lakes and smaller ponds and even gravel pits, and although most swans that we see are on fresh water many also live around estuaries, harbours and lagoons by the sea throughout Britain, except the far north of Scotland. They feed on aquatic and waterside vegetation so any quiet spot with a lush growth of plant material is ideal for them but they are also to be found in places where there does not appear to be much natural food available. Ideal foods include the various types of broad-leaved pondweeds and various species of duckweed. The duckweeds are particularly favoured by tiny cygnets as the small floating leaves do not have awkward lengths of stalk or root and are easily eaten. Common duckweed can be seen in shallower waters and often forms what

Male and female: adult pair.

looks like a complete green carpet across the water's surface. Juvenile cygnets and adult swans, however, are able to reach with their long necks three feet or more (about a metre) below the surface if they upend in the water to feed. Swans will also graze on grass, so anywhere that has grassy banks for them to climb out onto is desirable and attractive to them as it not only provides a source of food but a comfortable resting place as well.

Once a pair of swans have decided where they will live they settle down to establishing themselves in the area. Some swans may look for a mate as early as two years of age though they do not normally breed until the age of three to four years. In their first year together they will probably build a nest and even mate but they are unlikely to breed. All this activity helps to strengthen the bond between the two birds for the years ahead together: and swans remain together until one of the pair dies or they fail to breed. A nest used the previous year will be repaired and new

material added. Reeds and grasses are gathered from the immediate vicinity. For new couples, a nest must be constructed from the beginning and this can be a very painstaking process. It may take as long as two weeks of constant work before the nest is completed. The male collects the nest materials and passes them to the female. She arranges them meticulously to form a sturdy mound, which, as the years pass, becomes larger and larger. The nest may grow to be as much as three to five feet wide (1–1½ metres) and two and a half feet high (.75 metre). The female constructs the nest to form a shallow dip in the centre and lines this with soft materials and some feathers from her breast. This of course is where she will lay her eggs.

The ideal nest site is a secluded spot away from noise and disturbance and preferably surrounded by dense vegetation, such as on an island or in amongst clumps of reeds. A pair of local swans near where I live have a nest on a beautiful man-made lake which has all the facilities a swan could wish for. They chose to build their nest on an island surrounded by reeds and water iris. A nearer pair on a village pond had for many years built their nest by the edge of the pond. Within a

Nest building.

short distance from the bank was a small path and beyond that a row of houses near where children always played and cars parked but most people were very protective of them so they must have felt confident about this unusually exposed situation.

Swans may mate frequently from as early as February into the beginning of May. A charming and gentle sequence of movements precedes mating. The pair swim closely together and curve their necks, turning their heads from side to side together and their necks entwine. At intervals they dip their heads in the water. The male mounts the female's back and as mating takes place he holds onto her neck feathers with his beak. After mating the swans turn to face each other, and, with breasts together, their heads and necks stretched upwards, they rise together from the water, paddling with their feet. After this display they will swim and preen intensively for quite some time. The swans are likely to mate many times before egg-laying begins.

Pairs of swans will protect their territory and each other unrelentingly, the male swan being the more aggressive. This is most noticeable when the female swan is on the nest. During April and May, the process of egg production begins and the female swan lays her eggs. It can take more

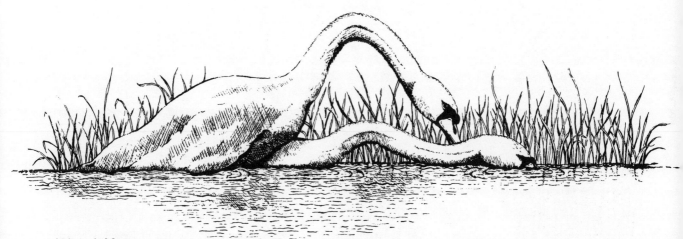

(Above) *Mating*.

(Left) *Courtship*.

than ten days for an average sized clutch to be completed. The eggs are laid one at a time on alternate days and there is an average of five to seven eggs in a clutch. The eggs are about 10 inches (25cm) in diameter and nearly 5 inches (12½cm) long. They are of an oval shape with a matt, slightly rough surface texture and the colour varies from bluish-grey to bluish-green. There are often faint scratch marks on the surface of the shell made by the swan's claws as she sits on the nest.

During egg-laying the female swan, known as the 'pen', will leave the nest to feed and preen as usual. When the clutch is complete, she remains on the nest, rarely leaving it, and incubation begins. The period of incubation does not start until the swan has finished laying all her eggs. If the female leaves the nest for a very short period, the male swan, known as the 'cob', will sit on the eggs until she returns to the nest. The eggs take thirty-four to thirty-six days to hatch, although it can be longer, as in the summer of 1988 when a Sunbury-on-Thames female incubated her eggs for fifty days and hatched eight cygnets. The eggs are constantly brooded by the parent bird and are regularly turned with the beak to maintain even temperature and healthy development within the

Rising out of the water after mating.

egg. Such constant attention to her eggs means that the female loses some weight and condition over the weeks between incubation and hatching.

While the female continues her long vigil the male is busy patrolling their territory, fiercely guarding his mate by keeping everything away. Any intruding swan will be repeatedly chased off, its invasion of an already owned territory being signalled by a variety of threat postures. The cob will continue to behave like this once his cygnets have hatched and whilst they mature. On land the aggressive posture entails the neck being held in an arched curve with the head pointing forwards quite close to the ground. As he approaches he snorts and hisses loud warnings as he raises his wings. When in the water his neck, with fluffed-out feathers, is held back on top of his body whilst the wings are raised over his back in an arched position. The swan will move swiftly through the water in a rather thrusting fashion and will pursue his enemy whichever way it turns. This particular threat posture is generally known as 'busking'.

A pair of swans may patrol quite a large area of river, sometimes as much as one or two miles, so this can make life very difficult for incoming swans without an established territory, especially in areas where suitable nest sites are rare. If

initial warnings are ignored the resident swan will become increasingly aggressive and may make a concerted attack on the intruder. Most swans have the sense to retreat before a serious fight ensues but on occasions during fighting a swan may sustain some injuries and in rare instances may be drowned by the dominant swan. This happens more frequently to ducks – although they pose no real threat the swan does not like them anywhere near. The pond near me supported a family of ducks and moorhens as well as the swans but they had to spend their whole time attempting to keep out of the male's way. The cob on this pond even spent hours chasing away groups of sparrows from the banks that had come to feed on leftover breadcrumbs.

Swans by nature are not aggressive, dangerous creatures. Left to their own devices they are gentle, caring birds. The defence of their territory and protection of mate and young is as intense as it is with other species, but the fact that the Mute Swan is Britain's largest water bird makes it perhaps more visually threatening to people.

Towards the end of spring and the beginning of summer the cygnets begin to hatch. At the end of incubation they make their first attempts to break

Nest changeover during incubation.

out of the egg. It can take a cygnet almost two days to emerge. It does this with the aid of an 'egg tooth', which is not a real tooth but is a hard prominence on the end of the upper beak which it

Threat posture.

Incubation.

(Right) *Newly hatched cygnets: the one on the right h*
just hatched.

uses in a hammer-like action to break the shell from within the egg. The egg tooth drops off soon after the cygnet has hatched. The cygnets are damp when they first emerge from the egg and are immediately brooded by the female so that their dense, fluffy down soon dries and helps to keep them warm. Although their down has a degree of protective oil to help insulate them they are still very dependent on their parents for warmth and protection and for helping them to feed in their first weeks of life. The cygnets all hatch within a short space of time of each other and the female remains on the nest watching over her ever-increasing family. They hatch with their eyes open and, although active, they do not leave the nest for the first few days. During this time the parents do not feed them but they survive on the nutrients of the yolk sac which they absorbed before hatching. After a couple of days they enter the water and swim well, even emulating the preening postures of their parents. The parents help them to locate food and tear up large pieces of vegetation for them. This way they quickly learn what is edible. At around the age of five days they will be spending most of their time in the water concentrating on feeding or resting on

Female swan with young cygnets.

grassy banks close to their parents. For the first month or so they will return to the safety of the nest at night with their mother.

Whilst the cygnets are still very young they may sometimes be seen riding on their mother's back, nestled between her wings. At this stage they are still very vulnerable and the parent's back provides a measure of protection from large, predatory fish such as pike and is a convenient place to rest if tired or alarmed. When swimming any distance the female often heads the family and, as the cygnets follow, the male, ever on the lookout for danger, swims behind the family.

For the first weeks of life the cygnets are a pale grey colour with silvery heads and underparts. Their fine, dense down is slightly coarser around the base of the neck and breast with longer filaments of down. Their legs, beaks and large feet are a mid-grey colour. In comparison to their relatively large feet their wings are minute and seem very out of proportion to their bodies. As the cygnets grow they rapidly behave like their parents and it is amusing to see them stand to try and flap their rudimentary wings. Looking at the stumpy wings of a young cygnet, it always amazes me that they will grow into the incredible wing-span of the mature swan.

By the age of four weeks the cygnets begin to

27

change colour slowly from a pale, silvery grey to a slightly darker grey and their bodies, necks, legs and beaks will have all grown considerably longer. The tiny wing shapes, although slightly longer, are the slowest part of their anatomy to develop. In the following weeks they continue to change colour to a grey-brown and take on a more tufty look as proper feathers begin to sprout. The cygnets are tremendously active, and having now forsaken the nest spend all their time with their parents engaged in preening and feeding. They will now be sleeping on the banks or islands at night. They constantly communicate with their broodmates by uttering soft whistling sounds. If

they become alarmed the soft sounds become much louder and at times quite frantic. The parents respond with a reassuring low grunting sound.

By eight weeks of age the cygnets have turned a darker brown and the wings are by now much more evident, looking rather like two very tufty epaulettes. Their tails have also grown and begin to take on a more pointed shape, though these are still very fluffy. Gradually the down is replaced by fully formed feathers and at three months of age only the tail looks a little untidy. During the next weeks the cygnets take on a mottled appearance and begin to look a paler shade of brown. This occurs as the white feathers of their eventual adult plumage grow through, gradually replacing the brown ones. As the summer lengthens the mottled appearance increases. The cygnets by now are large and strong and have equally large appetites. From four months of age the cygnets are able to fly, and can be seen exercising their wings; many do not fly for quite some months yet. At this stage they have the ultimate shape of the adult swan and although their beaks are still a dark grey, as are the legs and feet, they do have the black margins of the beak, but these are not yet fully

Ten-day-old cygnets.

developed. Their plumage continues to change until towards the end of the second year there is barely a trace of brown feathers. Their beaks remain dark grey until in their second year they gradually become tinged with pink as the grey fades. By now the characteristic markings of the skin around the base of the beak and on the beak itself are more accentuated. The colour of the beak deepens as the juvenile swan matures but even once the swan has attained all its white feathers the beak does not change to the orange colour of the adult until it enters into its third year.

The cygnets moult continuously into adulthood but the mature swans moult once yearly, towards the end of the summer. This can last for a month or more and during this time, as the swans are unable to fly, they are potentially very vulnerable. Adults with a family of cygnets moult at different times to each other so that always one of them can fly and protect the rest of the family. The female moults first and when regrowth of her feathers is complete the male then moults. Some of the cygnets may leave during the autumn but many stay with their parents until towards the end of winter. For the first few years of their lives the juvenile swans mostly congregate in non-breeding flocks, such as the ones I see in the South-East at

Hampton, Reading and Windsor on the Thames. In such a group they will find safety and are usually assured of a good supply of food by the many people that come to see them. They learn from one another as they mature, for in these groups there is even a form of hierarchy, the older juveniles tending to be more dominant. Within the flock they often form attachments to other individuals and, when old enough may have formed a strong enough bond with another swan to become an established pair and fly off to find their own territory.

There used to be a large, non-breeding flock like this at Richmond-upon-Thames but many became ill, largely from lead poisoning, and had to be removed for treatment. Those that survived were eventually taken to less hazardous areas whilst the few remaining moved of their own accord and joined other swans and cygnets at Hampton. A large flock now survives there quite well although this is still a high-risk area for them. Many people at Hampton keep a close watch on them and if any become ill they are rescued at the earliest possible moment; there is also a superb non-breeding flock at Windsor in Berkshire. These birds are well known to many people in the

Family with four-week-old cygnets.

Three-month-old cygnet preening.

area, particularly the owner of the café on the Promenade. He frequently has non-paying customers of the feathered variety loitering close by! This of course is a great attraction for the many tourists and summer visitors and information is made available to them concerning individual swans and their exploits. There is also a sizeable non-breeding flock at Reading.

Swans require considerable space to take off

and land. They are too heavy to fly straight up into the air so need an area of water large enough to use as a kind of runway in order to become airborne. They are the heaviest of our water birds and to become airborne they gather up speed by beating their powerful wings and paddling their feet in the water and gradually they are able to lift themselves into the air with the aid of extremely powerful wing muscles. On landing, their wing-beats slow down as they approach the water, at which point the swans' legs stretch forward and the large webbed feet act as a kind of brake as they spread out on contact with the water's surface. On dry land taking off is much more difficult; they are able to run in a fashion but require a strong headwind to assist them into the air. In flight a swan can reach speeds of up to fifty miles an hour but the average is around thirty miles an hour. Although swans are very strong fliers, they are also extremely prone to accidents for various reasons (see section on crashlandings).

In early autumn natural foods, such as the various waterweeds, are normally still available and if it remains mild well into this season the cygnets stand a better chance of gaining a good body weight before the cold weather of their first winter sets in. During late autumn the swans' supply of these foods rapidly diminishes and they

Family of swans with 8-week-old cygnets.

will begin to be more dependent on food from people. The cygnets have extremely large appetites and in preparation for winter tend to weigh more than most adults, so the whole family needs a considerable amount of food each day to survive. With an average-sized family this means a heavy demand on food availability within their territory. Whilst any warm, late autumn days and mild first weeks of winter continue this will increase the swans' chances to prepare for the intense cold to come.

As the first chilly, rainy days and sharp frosts arrive they will be noticeably more hungry. It is then time to begin offering as much food as possible. The depths of winter can prove very hard for all wildlife including the Mute Swan. Supplementation of a swan's diet during bitterly cold weather can mean the difference between mere survival, with loss of weight and condition, or even death, and keeping a large bird in almost peak health. As a grown swan requires at least eight pounds (3.6 kilos) of wet weight food daily it is not surprising to realize that, without human help in the worst of winter conditions, many swans might die. Often, the places where they live are sheltered in summer by overhanging branches

In flight.

and by bushes along the water's edge but in winter, with leaves from deciduous trees and shrubs gone, many sites become extremely exposed and the chill factor can be considerable. The main food available in winter is grass which can be grazed from nearby banks along rivers and ponds although there is limited nourishment on riverbeds. Even in the countryside there is barely enough to sustain them and a large percentage of their waking hours must be spent searching for food in order to survive; in urban areas natural vegetation is so limited that the swans need extra food. Many hours each day must also be spent preening as every feather must be in prime condition to ensure waterproof qualities for swimming and to provide insulation against the bitter winds and snowstorms of deepest winter.

Various types of food can be offered to swans, sometimes at little cost to the provider. Stale or surplus bread, preferably brown, can often be obtained from local bakers but it must be mentioned that some specialists advise that bread is bad for swans. Many suburban dwelling swans however seem to survive pretty well with this as a supplement to their diet and it would seem that in desperate situations they are better off eating some of this than not eating at all! Maybe everything in moderation should be the maxim here. In trying to get my swans in care onto solid foods after long periods of special tube-feeding, those suffering from degrees of anorexia for various reasons needed tempting with all kinds of foods. Amongst a pretty appetizing variety I offered was some bread. Many of the swans were from sub-urban areas and recognized bread as the most attractive food. In a small experiment offering only brown bread, this was often left, the swans seeming disinterested. On days where I offered brown and white bread as well as other foods they invariably scoffed all the white bread, left most of the brown and then went on to the other foods. I assumed this was because they were more famil-iar with white. Surplus leaves of lettuces and greens can often be obtained from local green-grocers and market stalls but in public places it is best to make sure first, with a small amount of greens, chopped and without stalks, that the swans you are feeding will actually eat these; no one will thank you for littering the banks and water with cabbages and brussel tops. Lettuce leaves are generally devoured straight away, but the appeal of other greenery differs from swan to swan. Swans also love mixed corn, flaked maize, layer's pellets and wheat which can be bought from pet supply stores, though I have found that wheat is often only sold by the whole sack. This

kind of food incurs expense, so it depends how keen you are on swans.

It is easy to see how much brighter and more active the swans are when the sun shines, even on bitterly cold days. During the long winter months they can often look quite dejected so it is impor-tant, if you know your local swans well enough, to be able to detect the difference between this and a swan that truly has the beginnings of an illness. Individual swans can be very different in their behaviour, so getting to know them really well can have great benefits in times of trouble for the swans.

During freezing conditions swans on small ponds may suffer from lack of water as these areas turn to ice. Not only do they need water to drink but, as they generally feed in the water, they have great difficulty in swallowing their food if it is not thoroughly soaked. Offering fresh water daily in some shallow container can be invaluable. This problem occurred locally near me but the situa-tion was easily resolved, as I shall explain later (see p.56). Being water birds they also automati-cally feel deprived by not being able to swim or preen properly.

Winter can be an important contributory factor

Underwater feeding.

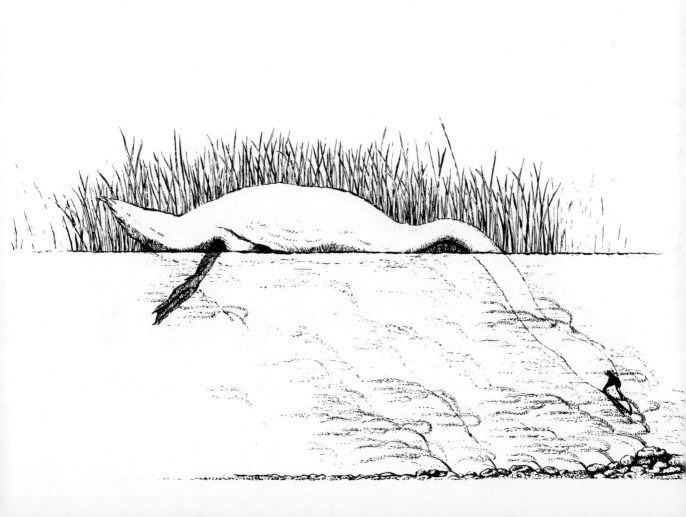

in the demise of old and sickly swans. Some of them may manage well with varying problems until the bad weather saps their energy and weakens their resistance. It is then that the vigilance of nearby people will be rewarded if they make an early rescue possible by alerting the relevant authorities. (Details of appropriate contacts are given later, see p.123).

By the end of winter most cygnets will have left their parents to make their own way in the world. Should a cygnet persist in remaining where it was reared, the parents, especially the male swan, may decide to chase it away. When this happens it seems rather sad to watch as a confused cygnet repeatedly tries to rejoin its parents, seemingly not understanding why the swan that so zealously guarded it during its growth appears suddenly to be so unfriendly. We watched this last winter as the male swan, still protecting three of his cygnets, repeatedly kept trying to drive the fourth one away. At this stage the swan no longer sees the maturing cygnet as one of his family but, with the promise of an approaching spring and with the adult's instincts turning to breeding once again, the cygnet is viewed as a threat. Possibly the cygnet we watched in this predicament was turning out to be quite a dominant youngster, and was probably a male.

At the end of winter, however, having followed our own particular local swans through all their possible problems of day to day survival we can hopefully see them safely into the dawning of a new spring.

Five-and-a-half-month-old cygnets.

2 Appearance

Both adult sexes appear identical with regard to markings and plumage although there is generally a noticeable difference in size. The male swan is usually larger than the female, has a slightly longer head and body, wider wingspan and the black, fleshy knob at the base of the beak is larger. It is more difficult to distinguish the sexes when seen individually, particularly if they are young.

The thick plumage is a pure, brilliant white, with the feathers lying sleekly in place, the underside of the body being covered with dense layers of feathers for buoyancy and insulation. The head and neck are covered with tiny feathers which lie smoothly back towards the body. When swans feel threatened or are unwell the neck feathers tend to take on a fluffed-out appearance.

The dark grey eyes have one eyelid, this being the lower lid; there is no upper eyelid. There is an inner eyelid which is a fine, transparent membrane similar to the 'third' eyelid of a cat. This transparent lid moves across the eyeball as the swan blinks and when it submerges its head under water. It helps to keep the eye surface moist and protects it.

The striking black markings of the skin around the base of the bird's beak continue along the edges of the beak to the tip on the upper mandible which ends in a black curved shape. This is sometimes called the 'nail'. The black fleshy knob of skin above the base of the beak grows in size as the bird matures and in a mature male can be quite large. The upper part of the beak is a rich red-orange colour which varies from bird to bird in intensity and the underside of the beak is pink and grey. Both edges of the beak are serrated and the pink tongue is ridged, which helps the birds to tear up vegetation when feeding. The black markings also extend from the base of the beak to the nostrils.

The swan has a long large body with a fairly short pointed tail and the sturdy black legs are set wide apart and further back than many birds, which accounts for its rather awkward, waddling gait when on land; but the legs are very powerful,

as can be seen from the strength displayed when swimming. The large, black, webbed feet have three long toes with nails pointing forwards and one smaller toe pointing backwards at the base of the leg; this toe is considerably smaller and of little use.

The wings are immensely strong and are a valuable part of the swan's ability to defend itself. The wingspan may reach up to 7 feet (2 metres). The long, outermost feathers are known as the 'primary flight feathers' and it is these feathers that, if they become damaged, lost or moulted, will prevent the swan from flying and will cause the bird to be grounded until new flight feathers have grown.

The weight of a male swan varies between 20 to 40 pounds (9 to 18 kilos) depending on age and size and total length can be up to 5 feet (1½ metres). The females generally have a smaller wingspan and weigh less.

Preening (oil gland at base of tail).

3 Ownership and Identification of Swans and Cygnets

The arrival of the Mute Swan in Britain is the subject of some controversy: some believe that it is indigenous to these islands, and others that it was introduced. However, since at least the twelfth century the swan has been cherished by man; the gentry have kept swans on their estates, partly for prestige and partly because the birds were a prized item of food. Swans have always been known as royal birds and originally, centuries ago, the Crown granted many important people licences to own swans. Today, however, this has been substantially reduced to only two other legal bodies of owners apart from the Crown, and applies only to swans resident on the Thames. These owners are the two livery companies of the City of London, the Worshipful Company of Vintners and the Worshipful Company of Dyers.

A major event in the owners' calendar is the ceremony of 'swan upping'. This is a centuries-old tradition of rounding up the breeding pairs of swans and establishing ownership of the new season's cygnets. On the River Thames, each summer in July, a flotilla of boats sets sail with the owners' skiffs each flying its official flag. Each owner has an official gentleman in charge. For the Crown is the Queen's swan keeper whilst the Vintners and Dyers each have a swanmarker. The Queen's swans are left unmarked; the Vintners' swans have one nick mark and the Dyers' have two. The cygnets are marked accordingly and where the parents belong to different owners the brood is equally divided, an uneven number sees the odd cygnet given the same ownership as that of the male swan.

The Queen's swan keeper and the swanmarkers perform many duties throughout the year. Each of them covers a specific area of the Thames and during the course of a year they rescue many sick and injured swans and cygnets.

Many swans and cygnets have identification rings on their legs and we commonly see two types. One, a narrow metal ring, is supplied by the British Trust for Ornithology and is therefore

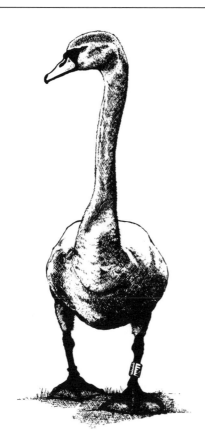

Darvic ring (on right) with BTO ring (on left).

known as a BTO ring. This ring has an identification number engraved on it and all details are recorded on the Trust's computers. It is not possible to read the number unless the swan is caught, but if one is found dead or injured and taken into care, the number should be reported to the BTO giving relevant details of the bird's condition and when and where found. This not only helps the Trust to keep its records up to date for study purposes but can provide the finder with some very interesting details. The Trust can tell approximately, if not exactly, how old the swan is, what sex and where and when it was first ringed. Sometimes the swan may have moved within a fairly small area but we often discover that they have in fact travelled quite some distance from where they were reared or lived when they were juveniles.

The second type of ring often seen is the wide ring known as a 'darvic' ring. This has large letters, or a combination of letters and numbers, engraved onto it, usually in black but sometimes in green. In the south of England we generally see this identification on a white background but the basic ring colours may vary around the country. These rings are used by various scien-

Swan feeding – showing darvic ring.

tists around the country who are engaged in official research and studies to do with the Mute Swan. Quite an informative picture can be built up over time; sightings of the swans are recorded by those involved in the work and include such details as movement between areas, matings, territories and breedings, accidents and illnesses. Many swans and cygnets that have been rescued and been in care for treatment are officially ringed prior to release and in this way their progress is monitored; it is useful to be able to find out their previous history if they should need to be cared for again. These large rings make identification from a distance very easy and are especially helpful if a particular swan is reported as being ill.

At Abbotsbury swannery cygnets have a small numbered metal tag attached to the foot (on the web) and many of the adults have a darvic ring.

Four-month-old cygnet: feathers around beak, chest and back towards tail begin moulting to white.

4 Swan Studies and Legislation

Mute Swans had been dying in increasing numbers for some years before the evidence of substantial numbers declining on the River Trent began to be queried. This was in the early seventies and by 1979 as deaths increased around the country there was also concern on the River Avon. In consultation with various authorities and at the request of the Minister of the Environment, the Nature Conservancy Council set up a working group to gather as much information as possible as to causes in the decline of the Mute Swan. All over the country exhaustive scientific studies were carried out, which included monitoring of breeding pairs, survival rates of cygnets, blood sampling, post-mortems of dead swans and many other aspects to determine exact causes and percentages of deaths in a range of areas. The country was divided into areas for this detailed research but rivers such as the Thames, Trent and Avon were individually studied because they seemed to be particular high risk areas. In 1981 the NCC published the report. Along with many other facts and findings, the report showed that lead poisoning was the single biggest killer of swans. Recommendations were then made for further studies to be continued and for the situation to be reassessed in 1984.

Many, many swans and cygnets continued to die and by the first few years of the 1980s it was estimated that between three and four thousand swans were dying each year. The great swan debate gathered momentum and as scientists all around the country were engaged in exhaustive detailed studies (such as the Edward Grey Institute at Oxford University, Ministry of Agriculture, Fisheries and Food), anglers, members of the public, conservation groups and those rescuing swans and treating them began to ask more and more questions and as often as not vociferously argued their points of view. A lot of publicity further raised countrywide concern and in January 1984 the MP for Richmond and Barnes, Jeremy Hanley, succeeded in procuring a debate in the House of Commons. As a result it

(Opposite) *Flying Mute Swan.*
(Overleaf) *Head of Mute Swan
and cob greeting pen.*

was proposed that a gradual phasing out of the use of lead weights (of those sizes most likely to cause problems to swans) should be encouraged on a voluntary basis, and that if this was not successful, legislation would perhaps have to follow.

The situation improved only very slightly and several more years went by whilst thousands of swans continued to die gruesome deaths. Many groups of investigating officers from different authorities continued to work unstintingly on the problem, and the National Federation of Anglers urged their members to take note of the scientific findings and were instrumental in testing non-toxic alternatives to lead weights being devised and produced by various manufacturers. They emphasized the Code of Practice drawn up for anglers and worked together with the scientists and alongside various conservation groups and those involved with the daily care of the rescued sick swans.

In 1986 further reports were studied and it was decided to introduce legislation in January 1987. This duly happened, as the voluntary ban had not proved successful.

In January 1987 the Control of Pollution Act (Anglers' Lead Weights) Regulations 1986, was introduced which made it an offence to import

At nest.

and sell split lead weights between the sizes of 0.06 gm (equivalent to no. 8 shot) and 28.35 gm (equivalent to 1 ounce). At this stage the use of these sizes of lead was not illegal and although the National Trust, the Forestry Commission and some local authorities had banned the use of lead, the government urged other water authorities to introduce byelaws to prohibit the use of these weights by the start of the following fishing season.

In June 1987 the Thames Water Authority and all other local authorities introduced the same byelaw which now prohibits the use of anglers' lead weights between the sizes of 0.06 gm and 28.35 gm.

Since 1987 there has been an encouraging decrease in mortality of Mute Swans from ingested lead weights, but there are still many swans continuing to be poisoned, suffering and dying as a result. This is undoubtedly because there must still be large amounts of lead weights in the environment, which, in areas with poor vegetation, get stirred up from activities on the rivers. Sadly, however, we are still seeing cases of birds caught up with fishing tackle which have the illegal sizes of lead weights attached, and many of the lead weights are new. Some people obviously choose to use something which is illegal despite the ample provision of viable non-toxic alternatives which are tried and tested by leading anglers themselves during production. They also choose not to care about the suffering they inflict or the bad reputation they are giving all anglers.

At the time of swan upping, figures on the Thames between Sunbury and Pangbourne seem to have remained stable, showing there to be 22 pairs of swans rearing 82 cygnets in 1987, whilst 26 pairs of swans were rearing 108 cygnets in 1988. Some casualties will doubtless have followed and not all cygnets will have survived to maturity. These figures have not included those pairs of swans which lost cygnets before July of each year. In the Thames area the latest figures indicate (inclusive of September 1988) that there has been a decline in the deaths of Mute Swans from lead poisoning from 60% down to 22%, which is from autopsy data. Similarly, there has also been a significant drop in the percentage of swans ill from lead poisoning when rescued, although some high risk areas still remain. Trends at the moment indicate similar improvements around the country.

Overall, the future looks hopeful for the Mute Swan as regards the fate of death by lead poisoning. Important studies are still being carried out by scientists, such as those at the Swan Study Group of the Edward Grey Institute of Field Ornithology at Oxford University.

5 Abbotsbury Swannery

The swannery at Abbotsbury in Dorset lies on the coast, south-west of Dorchester and west of Weymouth. It is situated opposite a large lagoon known as the Fleet which is separated by Chesil Beach from the English Channel beyond. Every year the swannery is visited by many people interested to see a place steeped in hundreds of years of history. It dates back as far as the eleventh century when it was owned by Benedictine monks. They kept and managed the large herd of swans as a source of food. Henry VIII dissolved the monastery and the land was eventually bought by Sir Giles Strangways and to this day it has remained within the care of the same family, descendants of the Earls of Ilchester. This is surely an amazing achievement and no doubt it is the fact that it has been privately owned by the same family for centuries which has enabled it to flourish unspoilt into the twenty-first century. Abbotsbury offers a unique experience to observe the Mute Swan at close quartes and in large numbers. In winter swans from other areas gather

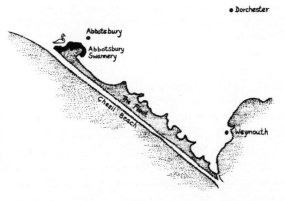

to over-winter on the Fleet and numbers may rise to as many as 600 swans. There is a marvellous information centre here which tells visitors everything they need to know about the place, the swans and their environment. The entire area has been designated a place of outstanding natural beauty.

The swannery first opens in May each year after the swans have nested and laid their eggs and closes in September after their annual moult as they make their way out to the Fleet for the winter. The gentleman who is in charge of the swans is known as the 'swanherd' and, together with a number of staff, he is responsible for the day-to-day running of the swannery. For those of us with more than a passing interest in swans it is a virtual paradise on earth. For some time I had meant to see Abbotsbury and when I first visited there in the early summer of 1984 it was everything I had imagined. Indeed my only disappointment was that I had to leave.

The picturesque walk from the car park increased my excitement with every step. For those less energetic in the hot, early June sun there was a horse and old-fashioned trap for hire to take one in style to the entrance gates. As I entered the swannery, a narrow path led us beside a small stream lush with vegetation and to my first sighting of the famous swans, a proud pair engaged in the task of teaching their young cygnets to feed. Further along, the path opened out to spread before me a panoramic view of the shore with the Fleet lying beyond. Abbotsbury is situated at the closed end of the lagoon so has some shelter and the swans are able to feed well on the abundant eel-grass *Zostera marina*. In harsh winter months the swanherd assists the swans by sup-

plying extra food such as grain. As the land is closed to the public in the winter we are only able to see it at its most beautiful but I was told that it becomes very exposed so it can be hard for the swans here, as in other places.

So breathtaking a sight was my first impression of this place that it lingers still in my mind's eye: swans were everywhere as far as I could see. It was incredible to know that so many hundreds of Mute Swans could co-exist so closely, particularly when one considers the rivalry for territories on inland waterways. A large proportion of the swans were swimming and feeding out across the Fleet whilst others closer to shore were preening and exercising their wings. Those on land were mostly dozing in the sun. I was particularly keen to see the numerous nests with the breeding females and their newly hatched young. Many of the nests are built by the swans very close to where visitors walk and although a small mesh fence separated us from the swans they took very little notice. I did not have to wait long before various females momentarily rose, giving us a glimpse of the beautiful downy cygnets sheltering beneath their mothers' feathers. Some of the nests had wooden stakes driven into the ground at wide intervals around them and we were told this is done to help prevent parts of the nest and the eggs

Swan resting.

from being washed away during heavy spring tides. Rushes for nesting material are also provided by the swanherd from the nearby reedbeds.

Another interesting aspect is the area where special cygnet pens have been created. A pair of swans live in each one whilst they raise their cygnets but they also act as foster parents to other cygnets. A certain number of cygnets are taken from a few nests on the open shore shortly after hatching and placed with their adoptive parents in the pens. Life in the open part of the swannery can be difficult for the cygnets as the protective parents sometimes argue and the cygnets may get injured. We were told that foxes are a problem and sometimes come in and take the cygnets, so managing them in this way helps reduce the overall percentage of cygnet mortality which, in the most ideal of situations, is naturally quite high.

I recently saw a programme which featured a piece on the Abbotsbury swannery. There was some stunning film of the swans flying in and landing on the Fleet but most enthralling was the sight of hundreds of swans eagerly clamouring to get near to the swanherd, John Fair. They had recognized him approaching and knew that the bucket he was carrying was full of grain. As he fed them, his dedication to his charges was obvious and I thought what joy and satisfaction his work must bring him. Here, the swans have none of the serious problems inflicted by man. No lead poisoning, fishing tackle injuries or vandalism to contend with, and with a longer life expectancy; this is more how life should be for the Mute Swan.

6 A Typical Local Pair

Until the winter of 1987/1988 there was a fine pair of swans on the pond at Lower Ashtead in Surrey, my local pond. They were quite a mature pair, had been on the pond for many years and managed to survive a variety of life's problems. Originally they had flown into Chessington Zoo but had caused so much upset to the birds already resident there that they were moved and brought to this pond. They settled in very well and every year saw them rearing a fine family of cygnets. Then, one spring all the eggs disappeared from the nest. People had various theories and it was reported that a fox had been in and made off with the eggs; this was very unlikely. I heard one gentleman say, and we all tended to agree, that it was a 'fox' of the two-legged variety. The swans did not breed again that year and when the next spring arrived the same thing happened again only this time a newly hatched cygnet also disappeared. There was obviously someone in the area who did not like the swans breeding and several rumours went around that people were complaining about the mess they made on the path. That was all speculation, but the local groups and residents remained extra vigilant and the following spring, the pair managed to successfully rear a brood of cygnets once again. The local authorities had fenced off the nest from the land side and sunk the fencing out into the water so this obviously made a difference to 'the fox'.

During the winter of 1985 the pond completely froze over and on one particular morning when I went to feed the swans they were nowhere to be seen. Eventually, after looking around for a while, I saw two large, white shapes in the distance across the common. The pair had flown off in a desperate search for water, and were in the process of wandering around the common in front of a row of houses when some children brought them out some water in a bucket. As I walked over to see what was going to happen the children told me the swans wouldn't drink. Together, we

Supplementary winter feeding.

decided that the bucket might be a bit too deep for them so I poured the water into the old washing-up bowl I had brought to put the food and water in for them back at the pond. The swans immediately became very interested in the sight and sound of running water and as we drew back to watch, the swans cautiously approached and then began to drink. The children were delighted and it seemed the swans were very much relieved. They drank more and then flew back to the pond and landed on the ice. This method of supplying them with water turned out to be a great success and they also ate extra supplies of food from this bowl. A gentleman who lived in a house by the pond took on the task of replenishing it with fresh water several times a day until the pond began to thaw. They became very spoilt swans; another local gentleman supplied a huge mound of straw on the ice and if we drove past at night we could see them both comfortably installed on the straw with their heads tucked under their wings.

During the following winter the pond froze over once again and the female swan became trapped in the ice. The local authorities were informed, she was freed and removed for a few days in care. She already had some arthritis in one of her legs and the ice had made this considerably worse.

She returned to the pond and although quite lame on the affected leg which caused her some difficulty in walking on land, she was fine in the water and continued her life on the pond with her mate as before.

In the spring of 1987 the pair prepared for a new brood and the warm days passed as the female patiently sat on the nest incubating. The new generation of cygnets hatched successfully and grew well as the next winter approached. Every year this brought anxious moments for those who watched over the pair and the impending cold weather revived the old fears for their safety. The female was still very lame but there was little that could be done for her and their territory on the pond was considered clearly the best place for them. All anyone could do was to watch and hope that nothing untoward occurred. In early December I thought she looked as though she might have lost some weight. It was not possible to tell without actually handling her and although she was very bright and eating well she just didn't look as good as usual. By now the pair were getting quite old and I began to have a nasty feeling that the female might not survive to see another spring day.

In the January of 1988 I learned she had been found dead by the pond. What we had dreaded for so long had finally happened. There was really nothing anyone could have done, but our immediate thoughts were then of how the lone male would react. At this time four of the original five cygnets were still at the pond and luckily he seemed so busy with his cygnets that he did not appear to pine over the loss of his mate. He was preoccupied with protecting three of the cygnets whilst persistently chasing away the fourth. He seemed to have taken a violent dislike to this cygnet and it was possibly a male and already showing signs of some dominance. The cygnets were by now well overdue for leaving their birthplace; they were generally manually removed from there as accidents often occurred when they tried to fly out, particularly as the road, which is very busy, runs right by one side of the pond. Eventually, by the beginning of spring all the cygnets had gone, one of them sadly had been hit by a car whilst trying to fly out and was so badly injured that it was rescued by the RSPCA Inspector John Paul and had to be put to sleep at a veterinary surgery. The male was now alone. What now we wondered? We did not have to wonder for too long; in March he too flew away, no doubt in search of a new mate. I would like to know where he is and what has happened to him; he was not ringed so we shall probably never know unless he returns to the pond with another swan. As winter approaches the pond is a quiet place without them and the empty nest a reminder of happier days.

7 The Damage We Do

Cygnet mortality is naturally quite high but in recent years many young swans have died between the ages of one to four years, which means that a high percentage of birds die before breeding age in particularly high-risk areas and although the Mute Swan as a species is highly unlikely to become extinct, the thousands of deaths which occur each year are intolerable when one considers how much suffering is involved. Our ability to stop natural causes of death may be limited but we can all help to minimize deaths from unnatural causes. The instances of particular causes of death vary in local areas and also vary greatly in different parts of the country. In each of the following sections I have given hints when applicable of ways in which you can help.

FISHING TACKLE

One of the most common causes of injury to swans and cygnets occurs from discarded items of fishing tackle, and accounts for a high proportion of rescue calls. This problem applies to all species of wildlife which live in or near areas which are fished and can result in distressing and sometimes serious injury. Although, over the years, the majority of cases I have seen involved swans, I have also seen seagulls, ducks and ducklings, moorhens, Canada geese, pigeons and grebes injured in this way.

Some instances are not too serious and can be dealt with on site but it is frequently difficult to catch an ensnared water bird which is in distress and not actually physically ill. Some swans may still approach to be fed and may be easily caught, but frequently when they have such a problem they become wary and tend to stay out of reach. It can sometimes take hours of patient waiting before they are persuaded to approach near enough. The rescuer may have to resort to the loan of a boat to enable capture on open water, but this in itself is likely to cause stress if a chase has to follow. If no boat with an outboard motor

Adult alert to danger.

is available it has sometimes been necessary to attempt rescue in a rowing boat. It is virtually impossible to keep pace with the swimming speed of a swan and a rowing boat is not easily manoeuvrable, but if there are any narrow backwaters to guide the bird into this can make rescue easier.

Tackle injuries if left unattended can have serious consequences. Swans sometimes do manage to free themselves of the problem, invariably after someone has run miles to the nearest telephone and usually just as the rescuer arrives. It can be very embarrassing and all one can do is to mutter profuse apologies. Occasionally strands of weed can be mistaken for fishing line so it is worth waiting a short while to make sure.

Hooks can cause severe injury depending on size and where in the bird they become lodged. I have seen hooks in birds ranging from very tiny ones to very large hooked pike lures. They are often swallowed whilst the birds are feeding; if caught in the mouth they may be fairly easy to remove but may tear the cheeks and tongue even before a rescue can be made. If actually swallowed they can be difficult to remove depending on how far down the oesophagus the hook has travelled before becoming embedded in the tissues. They are frequently a source of severe swelling and can cause nasty infections and abscesses as the metal of the hook begins to turn rusty.

Many hooks stuck in swans and cygnets and other birds still have the nylon fishing line attached and this can be particularly dangerous. If line is trailing from the hook the free end can become entangled in twigs, vegetation and other

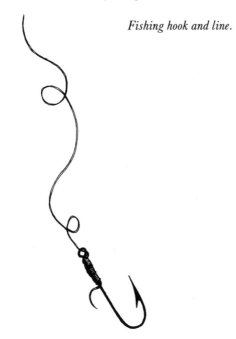

Fishing hook and line.

items in the water and is also likely to become snagged on overhanging branches from trees which trail on the water's surface. Alternatively, line is often caught around the bird itself and as the line is colourless this may not be at all noticeable for some time. As the line becomes tighter it is drawn beneath the feathers to lie out of sight and as the bird moves, the line acts like a cheesewire and begins to cut into the parts of the body around it. At this stage circulation is likely to be impaired and tissues start to swell as the line constricts. Swans have been known to lose parts of their beaks and have paralysed limbs. Hooks and line when swallowed obviously cause considerable distress; the birds can damage themselves further by struggling to get free and this leads to difficulty in feeding which can be the cause of starvation and eventual death. Various other items are often attached to line such as lead weights and seem to be as easily swallowed by swans as when the weights are individually picked up. Radiographs will often show the radio-opaque lead weights positioned in a neat line down the swan's oesophagus and into the gizzard, plus any hooks, whilst the actual fishing line cannot be seen as it is radio-lucent. Other items attached to the birds that I have seen include leger weights, reed inserts, balsa quills, pike lures and various floats and although the actual lengths of line vary there are often many feet of this attached to the bird.

In recent years there have been a number of organized clearances on rivers and ponds involving local councils, conservation groups and anglers who voluntarily gather up as much litter and harmful items of tackle as they can find. It is very depressing to see the volume of dangerous materials which are collected in a very short space of time. Fishing line can frequently be picked up along river banks whenever one chooses to look carefully along the water's edge and, even now, a considerable amount of lead weights are being found on line, of those sizes now prohibited. Of course some tackle is lost by accident because it gets caught on objects thrown into the waterways and cannot be retrieved – but plenty can be cleared up.

The amount of suffering that can be caused is immeasurable and those who discard tackle are rarely caught. Many anglers are responsible people and concerned about wildlife, taking a pride in preserving the environment they fish in, but, as often happens, the selfish and irresponsible behaviour of those knowingly discarding tackle gets everyone in fishing a bad name.

*

I feel very strongly about the damage fishing tackle does. It injures, maims and kills. However nice anglers may be (and many of them are extremely nice), they are responsible for causing the hideous suffering and death of many water birds each season; fishing tackle rates high on the list of hazards for wildlife dependent on an aquatic environment. A very high proportion of the swans and cygnets that I looked after had fishing tackle problems, whether as the prime cause of injury or as an added one to other reasons for rescue.

Not long after I had begun to take a particular interest in the care of swans I was able to go to the Zoology Department at Oxford University to visit Dr Mike Birkhead. He was at this time engaged in the official studies of the Mute Swan at the Edward Grey Institute and I took with me some dead swans which he was to post-mortem. He kindly took time from his heavy work schedule to show me a post-mortem in progress. There may sometimes be an aspect of the work that a veterinary nurse finds difficult to see: with me it's post-mortems. However, I knew that it was important that I should try and understand more of another aspect of the work I was interested in and it would be helpful for me to see the inside of a swan. In this particular case, the gizzard was

Old wooden float found in gizzard of swan at post-mortem.

dissected and there we saw a mass of tangled fishing line with several tiny pieces of lead weight attached and a wooden float three and a half inches in length. (The swan had actually died of lead poisoning and the post-mortem and subsequent analysis of bone, brain, kidney and heart would confirm this.) I took the items of tackle home with me and after some time spent unravelling the line I measured it and found it was sixteen feet in length!

The swans that were found dead or died in care in the following years continued to be post-mortemed by Oxford and with monotonous regularity, whilst reading through the results they sent me, there were details of various pieces of tackle that had been found within the swans. It is only the hooks and lead weights that show up on

radiographs or other pieces such as metallic objects.

Dr Jane Sears later took over the studies at Oxford and as recently as the summer of 1988 she post-mortemed a cygnet for me. I had been called to rescue an ill cygnet as no one else was available. The cygnet was separated from the rest of the family but the cob had still been trying to help it. When I arrived the cob was back with the family and after some time searching round the lake we found the cygnet lying on the shore by the water's edge. A pair of crows had attacked it and it was lying on its back but was still alive. I picked up the cygnet, which was only a few weeks old, and took it back to the veterinary surgery where I now work. The tiny bird had been very ill, it was extremely thin and was dying. It would not have survived for more than an hour at the very most and so it was put to sleep. The crows had been doing nature's work of disposing of an injured creature, its little eyes were bleeding and the skin was torn from its skull. The results of the post-mortem showed that eight strands of fishing line had become caught round its lower mandible and that the other ends had been swallowed. A large lump of undigested vegetation had become trapped on the line inside the cygnet's oesophagus and this had pulled the line so taut that the bird's neck was bent double. It had been unable to feed and had starved to death.

The next day the female swan became tackled. The anglers alerted the owner of the land and I was called out. I had my doubts about being able to catch the female as the male swan was likely to stay close to her and be very aggressive, protecting her and his cygnets. We began to feed them to get them close to the bank of the lake but the female stayed further away as she could not feed. Her beak was open from which fishing line trailed and she shook her head vigorously from side to side trying to free herself and we could see her tongue was bleeding. I knew I would only have one chance of catching her with my swan-hook (a specially designed metal loop on an extending

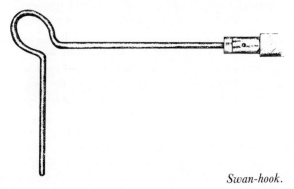

Swan-hook.

pole which is placed around the swan's neck in order to capture it and, used correctly, will not hurt the swan) and that if I missed she would come nowhere near us for the rest of that day. The male was by now getting very suspicious and began to hiss loudly; I'm sure he recognized a swan-hook when he saw one. The fact that they were both ringed obviously meant they had been caught before, and probably had not forgotten. As the female came just within reach of the swan-hook I managed to catch her and pulled her from the water. The male was by now furious and rose out of the water as he saw his mate drawn onto the bank. The anglers did a fantastic job of keeping him at bay whilst I removed the swan-hook from her neck and made a hasty retreat carrying her further up the grassy slopes. I set her down and looked in her mouth to see a large hook embedded in her tongue. One of the anglers very quickly removed the hook from her tongue with a pair of his forceps and we disentangled the swan from the long length of fishing line which had wrapped itself around her body under her wings. Within five minutes she was back in the water with her family and was steered speedily away by the male swan. At a later date the male swan also became tackled but managed to free himself before our local RSPCA Inspector arrived, but he checked the swan the next day as well to make sure it was still all right.

In the days when there was a flock of swans resident at Richmond-on-Thames I used to go frequently to see them. Whilst feeding them many other birds would gather round including the usual flock of pigeons. One particular time I noticed a pigeon which was having considerable difficulty in walking and could see that fishing line had become tangled round its feet and had tied its legs together. In vain I spent an hour trying to catch the bird but, having no net with me, it was impossible. The other birds kept getting in the way and eventually a dog rushed up amongst the birds and they all flew off. I waited for a long time but the injured pigeon did not return. Unless someone caught it the pigeon would likely lose its toes, and in this case probably both feet, as the circulation became restricted. We had many pigeons brought into the hospital with line round their toes and as the line is removed the toes often drop off. One pigeon that lived on the roof of the hospital had no feet at all but it managed to hobble around on its stumpy legs and had no trouble flying or feeding as it swooped down to steal food from the swans' dishes as we prepared them. I had wanted to save the pigeon at Richmond from such a fate.

I well remember a gentleman striding into the hospital one afternoon with an enormous herring gull tucked under his arm which he had managed to catch down by the River Thames. The gull was bleeding badly from its mouth and its beak was stuck open because an enormous pike lure was wedged in it. The lure was like a brightly coloured fish which is obviously what attracted the gull but there were two pieces of metal hanging from the lure which had three huge hooks on each piece and the hooks were embedded in the gull's tongue. Whilst we restrained the gull the vet snipped the hooks with wire cutters and the pieces were removed. After some treatment and time to convalesce the gull was taken to the coast and released.

On another occasion a Great Crested Grebe was brought in from the Thames. Yet again line was trailing from its beak but there was also something of a dark colour protruding from its mouth. As we examined the Grebe I was horrified to see that the 'thing' sticking out from its mouth was its tongue. It had become dried and shrivelled as the blood supply had been cut off when the fishing line tightened. The bird was very thin and we wondered how well it would survive if the line was removed. Having done this, part of the Grebe's tongue, about a third of it, had to be

Swan with cygnets.

amputated as the tissues were completely dead. Because the bird was so bright and active still we felt it was certainly worth seeing if it could feed now that the line and the useless part of its tongue were no longer in the way. I put the bird on the pond in the aviary and went to thaw out some whitebait, which we kept for occasions such as this. I threw the whitebait one at a time into the pond and as they drifted downwards the Grebe dived and greedily ate them. We did not know how much tongue a Grebe could lose and still be able to eat. The Grebe stayed with us until we were sure it had no problem with eating, that the rest of its tongue remained healthy and that it had gained enough weight. It was then released.

It can take many hours to rescue a water bird. In the spring of 1977 I was helping Tim Heron with some work for 'Swan Lifeline' when he received a call from a friend who said there was a tackled cygnet on the River Thames at Reading and that it was trailing a very long piece of line. We had the cygnet's darvic ring number so it would be easy to identify and we set off to the rescue. As it was a very active cygnet, about ten months of age, we realized when we got there that we were going to need a boat. The cygnet would not come in to feed with the rest of the flock and swam across to

Bill (see p.72).

the other side of the river. Luckily Tim knew some people who lived a short way from the bridge where the flock were most of the time, whose garden went down to the river and who had a boat. The gentleman and one of his sons came with us and after an hour or so they managed to persuade the cygnet to swim up a backwater behind a small island. With Tim and I on the island at one end with a swan-hook at the ready the men in the boat blocked off the cygnet's exit at the other end. Finally Tim caught the cygnet but not before he had ended up knee deep in muddy sludge at the edge of the island. With the cygnet safe Tim found he could not remove the hook on site so we drove to Steve Cooke's house. The large hook could be felt through the skin in the swan's neck and Steve made a small incision and removed the hook. It had already become rusty and an infection had begun around the site of the injury so the cygnet was detained on treatment until its wound had healed and was then released back to Reading. There had been about twenty feet of very thick line attached to the hook and the cygnet was very lucky to have got off so lightly. What particularly annoyed us was that it was at this time well into the 'closed' season. The hook did not look as though it had been lying around for several months before the cygnet came into contact with it and the line was not tangled in any way, but we could not tell for sure. The closed season unfortunately does not offer much respite from this hazard, although the instances are reduced during this period.

These are just a few examples of problems arising from fishing tackle; there are many more that I could write about and other people have dealt with far more serious incidents.

LEAD

Swans search for food along riverbeds and along the water's edge. As they feed they also search for particles of grit which they swallow. This helps to break down the tough cellulose of the plant materials they eat and therefore helps with the digestion of their food. Whilst swallowing the grit they are also likely to take in any discarded lead weights left by anglers. Various sizes of split lead shot match the sizes of grit a swan may search for and the lead, when left in the water, falls into the mud. Of course the swans are unable to distinguish lead from grit and herein lies the danger.

Once swallowed, the food, grit and any lead weights enter the gizzard at the base of the swan's oesophagus. The gizzard is a very strong, muscular organ which does the work of grinding down

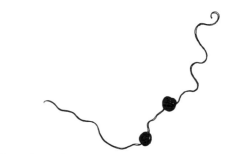

Lead weights on line.

the food with the aid of the grit. However, unlike the grit which eventually passes through and is excreted, the lead, being a very soft material, is ground down along with the food and gradually absorbed into the body through the digestive system.

Lead is a highly poisonous heavy metal. Absorbed lead can have severe effects on every part of the body. Particularly, it acts on the nervous system and a slow paralysis of the muscles begins which increases in severity the more

Lead poisoned swan: collapsed and unable to hold up head.

this toxic substance is released into the body.

Approximately three weeks after first swallowing lead a swan begins to show signs of illness. Various key abnormalities may be noticed. The prime ones have been well publicized and include the characteristic kink at the base of the swan's neck. As the condition progresses the wings droop, the eyes become dull and partially closed. The swan often drinks incessantly and appears to gape and salivate, shaking its head from side to side. As time passes the swan becomes more lethargic and usual behaviour patterns begin to change. Whereas it would normally approach to feed readily with other swans the ill swan begins to isolate itself, floating some distance away from a group. In the early morning and at dusk, whilst most swans are sleeping, an affected bird can often be seen floating aimlessly in the water. It progressively has problems swimming against any strong currents and tends to drift. As the

swan becomes more paralysed the neck droops further onto its back, if it has any degree of appetite left the swan is increasingly unable to feed itself or to preen properly so the feathers begin to take on an unkempt appearance. In extreme weakness and paralysis the bird is in great danger of drowning as its head falls closer to the water. On land, a swan in this state is often unable to walk or even stand; the tail and vent often have green staining as very watery diarrhoea is passed. With preening ceasing, the underside of the bird becomes waterlogged and with the massive weight loss incurred in many swans, not only is the breastbone more prominent and prone to abrasion but the swan is vulnerable to hypothermia as insulation is markedly reduced. Unless handled it is almost impossible to tell that a swan is losing weight, until it reaches a state of acute illness, as the thick feathers mask what lies beneath. Some swans continue to eat to try and alleviate their terrible hunger as their paralysed system digests less and less food. The paralysis can be so severe that any ingested food may remain in the oesophagus. With time, as more food is taken in it collects and becomes impacted further and further up the entire oesophagus. No nourishment is gained by the starving swan. This is a most unpleasant complication; however, many swans cease to eat before this stage is reached. In cases such as these the impacted food material can only be surgically removed.

As well as the digestive system, all vital organs including the heart, brain, liver and kidneys can be seriously damaged by this condition and from the onset of poisoning all these organs can begin to malfunction. Swans showing the most severe outward signs, however, can recover, whilst other swans showing less serious symptoms can quickly regress and die. Some of course are in such an appalling bodily condition and are so ill that a recovery would be impossible and in this situation the decision has to be made to let them suffer no further. In the early stages of treatment the ultimate results can sometimes be unpredictable.

Cygnets often contract lead poisoning whilst still very young. The closed fishing season begins in mid-March and lasts until mid-June; during the latter end of this period, the cygnets hatch. Theoretically, they should hatch into a relatively safe environment but they are often only a few weeks old when the fishing season resumes and many are seen to be ill not long after. With some lead weights already lying around it is possible for them to ingest these and become ill even before the season begins again.

Another theory, which is being scientifically investigated, is the possibility that cygnets hatch with congenital lead poisoning, that is to say, that if a female has a degree of lead within her before egg-laying commences, the lead, as well as being present in the tissues, can be stored in the bone and when calcium is released during the process of egg formation, lead could be released also and so enter the egg at the same time, thus poisoning the developing embryo.

Cygnets when first hatched have little resistance to illness, they are even more susceptible to hypothermia than adults and are very prone to pneumonia. A tiny cygnet which manages to survive treatment for lead poisoning can be at a severe disadvantage. It may suffer from slow general development which can result in stunted growth so that on reaching adulthood may be noticeably smaller than others of the same age.

Wry-neck is a neuro-muscular condition associated with lead poisoning. It is seen in cygnets and adults, although not every poisoned bird suffers from it. The neck is held in a permanently bent position with the creature unable to extend its neck. This means that the bird's whole stance is changed as it tries to balance in order to stand or walk and the body is held in an almost vertical position. It can be a long-term problem as, even if the rest of the bird improves, this effect can be permanent. Feeding and the ability to preen is severely affected and this is an exhausting and frustrating debility for the bird.

All this is physical proof of how these swans suffer. Of course we cannot be sure how they actually feel, and it would certainly help us if they could say. But it doesn't need much imagination to realize that their sufferings are no less unpleasant than for humans. Therefore, veterinary care requires a great deal of knowledge, as does nursing care; very important is an immense amount of thought and understanding of the swan's needs.

It is possible to treat lead poisoning very successfully following a treatment programme pioneered by veterinary surgeon Steve Cooke. I write from my own experiences during a particular period; since then Steve Cooke has continued to study this and many other problems involving swans and so treatment will have been updated. As each swan presents a different problem the treatment must be adapted for each bird. In some individuals damage to vital organs may not be reversible and, though they may appear to recover, these problems may remain masked for some time. Apparently recovered swans and cygnets have often prematurely died as a result.

Swans admitted with suspected lead poisoning are routinely weighed, X-rayed and blood sampled. The main purpose of X-raying is to establish whether there is any visible lead within the bird's digestive system. Sometimes if there is a massive amount of lead weights within the swan it is necessary to use an endoscope to locate the pieces and remove them immediately before they poison the bird further; this was carried out at 'Save Our Swans' by Steve Cooke. The absence of lead weights on a radiograph does not automatically mean the swan is clear, so it is always necessary to take a blood sample from the bird to be sent off for analysis.

The blood is tested for lead levels and also gives an indication of any anaemia and the percentage of red blood cells present. In many swans and cygnets it is necessary to add an iron supplement to their feeds as lead interferes with the production of red cells. The results, although showing what the tissue lead levels are at the time and giving an indication of the extent of the swan's illness, do not exactly describe the bird's actual state. Sometimes one is suddenly faced with a bird that is far more ill than one had originally

A normal, healthy swan chasing off intruders to territory; a sick swan lacks the will to do so.

thought. It is therefore important to re-X–ray and re-blood sample as well as checking on the weight.

Once lead has been absorbed into the body it cannot be excreted without the administration of special drugs. This consists of injections and in the latter stages of treatment tablets are given. These particular drugs are known as 'chelating agents' and, in simple terms, they combine with the heavy metal, in this case lead, into a form in which it can be excreted from the body. The injections eliminate the lead from the tissues and the tablets eliminate it from the bone. Other injections are given also to help with vitamin deficiencies, to help build up muscle after the effects of muscle wastage, antibiotics to guard against secondary infection and others to help with any malfunction of the heart. Tablets also are sometimes given for heart problems. Other oral medication is often necessary with preparations given to help with the replacement of mineral and vitamin deficiencies and with the malabsorption of fluids. Many swans and cygnets exhibit signs of dehydration which in most cases are not difficult to rectify after a period of oral therapy but in some particular cases it is necessary to give swans intravenous fluids in the form of a glucose saline drip.

When the digestive system is severely impaired it is necessary to force-feed swans and cygnets, which involves passing a special tube down the swan's oesophagus to its stomach and then syringing a liquid food mixture down the tube. It does not hurt the swan, and although it cannot be a particularly pleasant experience, they soon become accustomed to this. Tube-feeding of anorexic swans has proved many times to be a real lifesaver. The basic liquid feed consists of a mixture of Complan to which any other relevant preparations are added; the percentages of the mixtures were all worked out for me by Steve Cooke and all the swans being fed in this way were given this three times a day. This routine needed to be continued for some considerable time even when the birds had begun to eat for themselves. At the beginning of the tube-feeding some of the food would often pass straight through undigested, but as the birds improved and their digestive systems became less paralysed more of their food was utilized by the body. When the swans began to eat, their weight often remained stable but they would not be taking in enough food to sustain them without tube-feeding. Throughout this period tube-feeding serves to maintain an already vastly depleted body and it is often some months before considerable weight gain is noted.

In the process of making good recoveries and whilst treatment is gradually reduced it is necessary to look after the swans for quite some time whilst they regain condition and strength. Birds that have been seriously ill would be unlikely to survive fending for themselves immediately after finishing treatment and one has to be as sure as is possible that complications are unlikely to arise, so sometimes a fairly lengthy period of rehabilitation may be required. The swans and cygnets I treated went to Steve and Zyllah Cooke's for their rehabilitation. Weighing of the swans is always important and the swan needs to reach a decided target weight before release and it must also have plumage in good, waterproof condition before its release. Offering the right kinds of foods, providing suitable bathing facilities and shelter as well as providing as near natural surroundings as possible are important for recuperation. It helps them to have the company of other swans. It is also important to keep them clean; in the case of those birds which are too ill to help themselves one has to be careful not to add to stress, but washing keeps them happier and more comfortable. Physiotherapy can be a time consuming but vital part of a swan's recovery in order to encourage the regeneration of wasted muscles.

*

In the autumn of 1981 a large male swan was brought into the hospital. He had lived for many years on Barnes Reservoir in South London. With his mate he had proudly reared generations of cygnets. When his mate died many female swans flew into the area at intervals but none of them was acceptable to him. Eventually, a female swan flew in which obviously had all the attributes that Bill required and she stayed to become his mate. The swan became known as Jill and together they continued their lives until one day she too died. It was not until Bill became ill that it was realized what the probable cause of Jill's death had been. The reservoir had been a well protected haven for wildlife, and still is to this day, but in those days some fishing was permitted and it was this that led to the swans' downfall. Bill had become lead poisoned.

Lady Follett and George Rapkins who run the Barnes Wildlife and Animal Welfare Group had devoted many years to the wildlife in the area. Bill and his successive families had spent many hours in their company and trusted them completely. Because they knew Bill so well they were able quickly to spot any problems and one fateful day, all was not well with Bill. Although he was by now known to be quite old he was definitely ill so

he was removed from the reservoir and taken into care at the RSPCA.

The usual procedure was followed when Bill was admitted; having logged his BTO ring number, I sent the details off to be recorded. His ring number identified him to be over an amazing sixteen years of age. In his youth he had been ringed at Ware in Hertfordshire. The secret of his long life certainly lay in the fact that he had acquired himself 'guardians' who were totally dedicated to the welfare of him and his family. The fact that he was so used to human contact undoubtedly helped enormously with his change of lifestyle and his 'guardians' came in regularly to visit him. He was very thin when he arrived but ate well from the beginning; even so, this was monitored carefully in case he needed additional tubefeeding. His treatment for lead poisoning was begun immediately and he started to respond well. Added to the problems of this debilitating illness he also had arthritis in his legs, which, made worse by his poisoning, meant he couldn't stand or walk properly. By the time he had been in a week he was beginning to walk but very badly, so he was put in a bath daily for physiotherapy; this also kept his tail and vent clean which became very soiled as he was sitting down most of the time, and it encouraged him to preen.

By now, some of the days were very cold and damp and besides being kept in at night he sometimes had to stay in for part of the day as well. Within a few weeks he was much stronger, was still eating very well and putting on weight at a surprising rate. We could no longer feel such a prominent breastbone and the strength in his muscles was much better. His overall condition continued to improve but he still had recurrent bouts of lameness and his leg joints became hot and swollen. Although treatment at regular intervals reduced the frequency of this problem, and Bill managed very well, it was clear this was going to be a permanent disability.

Towards the end of intensive treatment we began to think of his long term rehabilitation. There was a lot to take into consideration. He had by now gained almost ten pounds in weight but the fact that it was the middle of winter and he was very old meant he would need easy access to lots of food. He also needed exceptionally safe surroundings at night because of his reduced mobility; in view of the fact that he would almost certainly need treatment from time to time for this arthritis, he needed to be accessible. In consulta-

'Busking' cob protecting territory; female is on the nest in the background.

tion with Lady Follett and George Rapkins everyone concluded that he was unlikely in the long term to cope on his own, so we regrettably had to decide that he could not go back to his old haunts on the reservoir. As his treatment for lead poisoning was gradually reduced we set about finding suitable accommodation for Bill and shortly the ideal place was located.

Bill was transferred to a farm near Dorking in Surrey. Many other birds had found refuge here, some were previous in-patients of the hospital, including various hens, Aylesbury ducks, mallards and a Canada goose called Gertie who was no longer able to fly. They all amiably shared the facilities of ample food, grassy banks and a lovely pond and were put away at night in case the old fox came around. Bill arrived here in the following January and settled in immediately. He had a ramp built for him so that he could easily get in and out of the pond and even had his own special 'house' to retire safely to at night. I kept Lady Follett and George Rapkins informed of his progress.

I had promised to take them to see Bill in his new home but with the pressure of work I was not immediately able to do this and one morning at the end of January I received a phone call at work to say that Bill had died. Right up to the end he had been very bright, active and eating well and nothing wrong had been noticed. I had the unpleasant task of breaking the news.

Although the degree of lead poisoning had not been as severe with Bill as in many other swans we've treated, the post-mortem carried out at Oxford showed that the effect of lead poisoning was the primary cause of death. Due to his age he had been at a considerable disadvantage in conquering the problems of being poisoned; at least he had received an immediate rescue and prompt treatment as soon as symptoms appeared and had once again enjoyed life before his quick departure from this world. Bill had not suffered a slow, lingering death like so many other swans.

One October morning Bill Colley, the Vintners' swanmarker, arrived with a young female swan which he had been called to rescue from the River Ember at Esher in Surrey. She was unwell and he suspected that she was suffering from lead poisoning. There were no identification rings on her legs but from her plumage and the colour of her beak we could tell she was only about two years old. This was the swan I named Eleanor and was the creature which, unknown to me at this time, was to have such a profound effect on my life.

Once she was admitted and a record card made out with all relevant details, I carried her to the X–ray room. The developed radiographs showed that there were five pieces of lead present in her gizzard. They varied in size and two pieces in particular were very small and it therefore appeared that these had been partially digested. We could not tell how much, if any, had been completely absorbed previously so the next routine step was to take a blood sample from her. The sample was immediately sent away for analysis. I also made a slide which under the microscope showed the presence of damaged red blood cells. Due to the positive identification of lead on her radiographs I began the swan's treatment without delay.

She weighed 14 pounds (6½ kilos) when she was admitted and, for her size, she was underweight. She felt extremely light and her breastbone was very prominent. There was obvious muscle wastage in her legs and wings but, although weak, she was able to hold her wings up and could stand and walk reasonably well. Her neck and head were held in a fairly normal position but the 'kink' at the base of her neck was pronounced. Eleanor, althoughly clearly ill, showed no severe symptoms and I was quite hopeful of a recovery at a future date. Because of her weight loss and poor condition she would be susceptible to feeling the cold. Her tiny neck feathers had the fluffed out appearance seen in lead poisoning, tail and wings were unkempt and the covering of feathers underneath the body was not completely waterproof. She had obviously not been preening properly.

Noticing all these things about Eleanor, I was anxious to see if she had a reasonable appetite, so after her first set of injections I carried her out to the aviary to join the other swans I was looking after. I was disheartened to quickly realize that she was not going to eat. I allowed time for her to settle in after being snatched from the freedom of the outside world but she still stood quietly by whilst other swans greedily tucked into the containers of food. This should have provided her with some encouragement but all she did was drink a few sips of water every so often and shake her head. At least she was not dehydrated, which would have complicated things considerably. With a delay only short enough to convince myself that I had another anorexic swan on my hands, I went off to the kitchen to mix up some Complan in order to tube-feed her. With the rest of her treatment she was tube-fed three times a day on Complan with the necessary additives such as an iron supplement and for several weeks her weight remained the same. No better but at least no worse. It was early days.

I had once rescued a swan that had such a severe impaction that food lay packed solid from the base of its oesophagus right up to the top of its throat. This pathetic creature, an adult swan, weighed seven pounds. It was no more than a floating skeleton, weighing less than an average sized domestic cat. The real horror of this experience was that it was still alive. There was nothing I could do for this swan but put it out of its misery. Thinking of that poor swan, how relieved I was that Eleanor was at least free of this problem. She digested her feeds quite well and remained stable. Actually feeding her presented no problems at all as she was such a delightful patient, seeming to sense I was trying to help her. In the early days of feeding her I had noticed a small swelling under her tongue but to begin with could see no cause for this. The area was sore and ulcerated. Further examination at her next feed revealed something like a colourless thread protruding from the edge of the wound. I gently tugged at this with a pair of forceps and after a few seconds pulled out from under the inflamed skin a small, tightly packed ball of nylon fishing line with four very tiny pieces of lead attached to it. I therefore X–rayed her head and neck to make sure no hooks were embedded anywhere. Maybe this was why she hadn't wanted to eat? Not so. Within a week the ulcer had healed but still she refused to eat.

As the days went by Eleanor settled well into her new surroundings and became brighter. Through all the handling during her treatments she remained the trusting, sweet-natured swan she had first appeared to be. As swans and cygnets improve, their very different characters become noticeable and they are not always so co-operative as time goes by. Eleanor remaining placid in this respect, grew more active, taking an interest in things around her and began swimming and preening with renewed vigour.

It was not until the twenty-eighth day of intensive care that Eleanor decided finally to take her first beakful of food. The news spread pretty quickly and I celebrated. I was so relieved and excited. Over the weeks the feeding regime had kept body and soul together, though at her last weighing she had actually lost three pounds which was a great worry to me. Despite the fact that she had begun to eat, she still had to be tube-fed to ensure that no further weight loss occurred and to supplement the meagre amount she was eating herself. The consumption of Complan was enormous since we were caring for many swans and cygnets, and I wondered if the sales assistants in the shops were curious where it was all going. I certainly didn't look as if I was taking it myself. Eventually we got in touch with the manufacturers who kindly delivered a consign-

Preening.

ment every so often to Windsor and Steve and Zyllah and myself would split the delivery.

Eleanor continued to eat by herself and with her extra three feeds daily from me she regained the lost three pounds' weight and very slowly began to gain a little more than her original admittance weight. At this stage I was more than hopeful that she would make a full recovery. Dr Mike Birkhead from the Swan Study Group at Oxford University called in one day; he visited the hospital from time to time to collect any swans that had died. I took this opportunity to ask him about Eleanor and he said she was in quite a bad way, judging by her blood results, and that she was suffering from long-term chronic lead poisoning. My eagle eye therefore continued to detect the minutest change in her as I resolved that her life would not end if there was the slightest chance that I could save it.

The outward signs seemed to be encouraging, except for a few days when her breathing was not very good and I feared she had a heart problem, but after some days of additional treatment for this, things improved and whilst routine continued my – by now rather special – swan was evidently enjoying life once more.

One mild afternoon in November we saw Eleanor building herself a 'nest'. She had pulled mounds of bedding material from under the shelter in the aviary and was busy arranging this around herself. As a piece of swan behaviour it was fascinating to watch but it also became extremely amusing. This activity had encouraged the other swans and juvenile cygnets to copy her. They placed themselves behind her and each other. The swan immediately behind Eleanor began to remove some of her nest material and arranged it around itself and in turn all the others did exactly the same, taking bedding from the one in front. This chain-gang activity could have been watched for hours if only I'd had the time. Eleanor kept feverishly piling bedding around her whilst the smartest swan at the end of the line finished up with a larger nest than all the others! This kept them occupied for most of the afternoon.

Eleanor and I became closer throughout these days and I spent as much time as possible with her, the rest of my work load permitting. It wasn't that I didn't care as much for all the others but that there was a great affinity between us. Although always gentle she was not keen on close contact with other people; simply she knew me best, but she delighted me one day when she 'posed' beautifully for a newspaper photographer who stood very close to us. During the day I would always call to her if I passed the aviary in the course of other work. She would look round, point her head upwards and reply with a series of low, grunting noises. At first I thought it was coincidence so I tried this every time, and every time she would reply. One morning I saw her look up to the sky, her head tilted to one side, as an aeroplane flew over. No doubt she wished she too could be free to fly.

The routine of her care was combined with her being let out into the aviary in the mornings and being brought in again for the night. By now the evenings were chilly and the nights far too cold for her to remain outside as she was still underweight and would run the risk of hypothermia. She would get excited when carried to the door in the mornings and as I put her down and opened the back door she would waddle out ahead of me to the aviary gate and wait for me to open it. Then she'd proceed with a speedier waddle into the pond for much needed exercise followed by intense preening.

In the evenings when I brought her indoors, she would freely walk into her kennel and settle down. I found this remarkable as no swan likes to be confined particularly when as bright and active as she had become. This was the best part of the day, time to sit with her and continue to encourage her to eat. As a special treat, a large lump of Madeira sponge was to act as enticement mixed in with her other food, but this was greedily snatched from me before I could fully remove the wrapper. She did not want to give this up but having got the wrapper off the cake I handed it back to her whereupon she snatched at it, plonked it in her water bowl and devoured every crumb.

One evening, my work finished, I sat with her for a long time. As I stroked the innerside of her neck, with her beak resting in my other hand, Eleanor went to sleep. I wondered how long she would stay like this before she realized what she was doing. An hour later, with Eleanor's head still resting in my hands, I decided it really was time for me to leave and go home. She had occasionally opened one eye, looked at me and having taken a deep breath and a sigh closed her eye and dozed off again. Normally, with wild creatures one wouldn't make a habit of this kind of thing as it does them no good if they are to be released into the wild unless they have adequate rehabilitation away from man, but as the swan is semi-domesticated anyway this would in no way endanger her chances of survival back out on the

Preening.

80

river. As I got up to leave I gently moved her head and slowly tucked it under one wing. She opened her eyes, looked at me and then snuggled her head further into her feathers and went back to sleep.

Another month went by and Eleanor continued to do well. Various 'off' days found me having a quick panic but generally everything was satisfactory. A little more weight was gained and she was a lot stronger. By now, well into December I felt the last two months of exhausting work was beginning to pay off.

Suddenly one night, shortly before Christmas, Eleanor died.

I felt real grief for the death of this beautiful creature that had enriched my life and from which I had learnt so much. I went through all the 'if onlys' in my mind and wished for weeks that I'd been with her when she died. It probably made no difference to her but it did to me. It was a brave friend on duty who rang to tell me the news and I drove to the hospital. Eleanor's lifeless body lay in her night-time kennel. Although she died five years ago, memories come flooding back and it seems as though it was only yesterday.

It was a beautiful, sunny mid-June morning, the kind of day that lifts one's spirits. Even the recovering swans in the aviary seemed to look as though all was right with their world. They were noticeably brighter and as the sunlight shone on the pond through the trees they were energetically preening after their early morning swim. My sense of calm and pleasure at seeing them improving from their various illnesses was not to last for long, for shortly I was to have another casualty to concern myself with.

During the course of the morning, Mr Harold Cobb, the Dyers' swanmarker arrived and as I went to meet him I saw that he was holding a small, fluffy grey bundle in his arms. This was Rosie, a beautiful cygnet of about three weeks old.

The swanmarker had rescued the cygnet from Sunbury-on-Thames where a concerned member of the public had noticed something unusual in the little cygnet's behaviour and had called for help. The cygnet had been with her parents and the rest of her broodmates but she was clearly ill and had to be removed without delay.

When placed on the ground she was able to stand but the posture was very unusual and it was evident that the cygnet could not balance properly. Her neck was held in an awkward position so, in order to compensate for this, the cygnet had to

Rosie, showing wry neck due to lead poisoning.

hold her body in an almost vertical position. During this she would flutter her tiny wings to assist her to stand. The neck was bent back in a stiff curve resting on the body. All these features produced great problems in walking and particularly in feeding. The ultimate result was that the little creature fell over onto her back, and, with her legs flailing in the air, was unable to right herself. Time and again valiant attempts were made to walk normally and when the inevitable happened, the normal cygnet calls of gentle whistling noises would turn to frantic loud calls for assistance. Once picked up and on her feet again, with confidence renewed, the courageous cygnet repeatedly tried to behave like the normal bird she felt she ought to be.

Rosie appeared to have the condition known as wry-neck, a problem often associated with lead poisoning. It clearly caused the cygnet much mental distress and physical exertion. Her parents could have done little to help her. As well as being at risk of starving to death, she was also at risk from hypothermia because she couldn't preen and therefore oil her down and in the water would

have been at great risk of drowning. On further examination Rosie's bodily condition was actually very good, her eyes were bright, her weight quite good and she was very lively. When offered food and handfed the cygnet ate readily. She also passed normal motions. I took the little cygnet to be X–rayed and when developed, the radiographs showed no obvious signs of abnormalities, neither did they reveal that any toxic objects had been swallowed. However, due to the presence of what appeared to be a neuro-muscular disorder I took a blood sample from the cygnet which was immediately sent off for analysis by the Veterinary Investigation Centre's laboratory at Loughborough. Whilst waiting for the results and having assessed the cygnet's condition carefully, we began some basic treatment. At this stage medication was kept to a minimum, as until we had a more positive indication of the cause of the cygnet's illness, we did not want to give any drugs unnecessarily.

Rosie continued to feed well, remaining bright and alert; she enjoyed a comfortable compound erected in the warm sun during the day. All food was greedily welcomed and the supplies of duckweed I collected and brought in were devoured with relish. I continued to support the cygnet whilst she ate and to keep her warm and dry after feeding and preening. If I disappeared Rosie would begin to call loudly until someone was again in view; security restored, the cygnet would become more settled. The daytime compound was outside the window of the ward I was working in looking after numerous cats, so it was easy to keep an eye on the cygnet all day whilst doing other things. After a mere two days I had naturally become very fond of this dependent creature.

On the third day, early in the morning, without any warning Rosie suddenly collapsed and despite my desperate attempts to help her, within a few minutes the cygnet took her last breath and died in my hands. For a while longer I stood and looked at this beautiful cygnet and thought how it seemed to be such a terrible waste of life. When taking on the care of very young dependent mammals and birds a routine is quickly established and one's days and nights are automatically tuned to the frequency of attention that is required. Throughout the rest of my work for some days I still kept thinking that there was something else I should be doing and it was then that I realized that the passing of Rosie had left a void that took some time to fade.

Later, on the same day that Rosie died, the blood results arrived and I was grieved to see that the lead levels in the blood were found to be ten times higher than normal. Whilst the cygnet had remained bright and with such a strong will to live I knew, however, that we had been justified in giving her a chance.

Although these stories of lead poisoning have sad endings, happily many swans do recover as a result of the treatment.

OIL, DIESEL AND CHEMICAL POLLUTION

Various types of toxic materials enter rivers, their tributaries and backwaters as waste products of industry, sometimes from boats and by deliberate dumping. Industrial chemicals, diesel and sump oil all have considerable devastating effects on wildlife. They can poison everything from vegetation to fish, mammals and water birds.

Oil adheres to the feathers of water birds which makes the plumage stick together and the birds are then faced with a loss of waterproofing qualities which means they are no longer buoyant in the water and will sink. They will also begin to suffer quickly from hypothermia as the insulating properties of their feathers are impaired. The birds will immediately start to preen in an attempt to rid themselves of the problem and in doing so may swallow large quantities of oil. This

has very damaging effects on the digestive system, causing severe inflammation and can also damage organs. It is necessary to give oral medication, usually in tablet form, straight away and this is given until signs of oil being passed in the motions have stopped. Oil can cause severe skin irritation and around the beak and face often produces shrivelled, dry skin which eventually cracks and peels if it is not lubricated. The eyes are also often seriously affected, becoming very inflamed and sore and eye ointment may need to be applied three or four times a day. Oiled birds need quiet, warmth and food when they are first taken into care but must not be given access to water except for drinking and feeding.

The actual process of cleaning a badly oiled swan is a matter on which I am ill equipped to report; I know from bitter experience that this should never be attempted by anyone who has not been expertly trained. There is a standard set of guidelines laid down, which gives precise instructions in a list of do's and don'ts but even following these it is not as simple as it may seem. There has been considerable research done by Newcastle University and the RSPCA has a Wildlife Field Unit in Somerset specially equipped for this purpose. They, or the Wildlife Department at RSPCA Headquarters, Horsham, should be contacted when the need arises.

The problem of swans becoming covered in diesel is fairly common: the swan doesn't appear brown, as when covered with sump oil, but can have a noticeable lack of waterproofing and a distinctive smell. Most of the swans I've been involved with did not need cleaning as the advice was to let it 'weather off' but this can take some weeks during which time the swan will not be fully waterproof and should not have access to water where it can swim. All water birds must be totally waterproof and tested in a confined area before they are released, to make sure they do not become waterlogged and sink. Swans suffering from the effects of diesel have the same problems with damage to their eyes and skin and have also to be given oral medication. Many of them exhibit varying degrees of baldness on the head and neck a few weeks after coming into contact with the diesel.

Chemical pollution of the waterways is often more difficult to detect, and although the death of fish and plants is evidence of a serious problem the waters may be chemically contaminated to a degree which is not obviously visible; even so this will be having an effect on all species of wildlife in an accumulative way, by slowly poisoning them and so inhibiting growth and reproduction and by reducing natural foods. Water authorities regularly monitor conditions but they should be notified if anything is suspected.

One March a female swan of about two years of age was brought in from the River Thames at Hampton. She had been rescued as she had become covered in diesel and was therefore rather unwell. Although her appearance did not look critical she obviously needed attention and even though bright in herself, she was noticeably affected by her accident. It soon became apparent that it was not only the diesel which was troubling her, something else about this swan did not seem 'quite right'. As a precaution she was X–rayed but nothing abnormal showed up. I took a blood sample from her and sent this away for analysis.

We bathed this swan as she was clearly extremely agitated. The bath was very successful and also removed most of the terrible pungent smell. Once over this ordeal she looked considerably better and happier. At this stage it was wise to assume that she would have swallowed a degree of diesel so she was given a quantity of soothing liquid medicine to help line her digestive system and reduce the irritation to the tissues. As

Loss of feathers on neck due to diesel.

her head had come into contact with the diesel her eyes were already very sore and red so I began to apply eye ointment four times a day. The surface of her beak and the black skin surrounding it had begun to shrivel and crack so I rubbed Vaseline well into these parts which helped to lubricate and keep the skin supple.

This swan's weight was good and although she would not eat we presumed it to be the effects of the diesel but several days later the results of her blood sample arrived back and we discovered that she had a degree of lead poisoning. She began treatment for this and I also tube-fed her. She picked up very quickly and by the end of her first week in care she was eating very well and from then on went from strength to strength. Her improvement really was miraculously fast.

She became waterproof and the overall look of her became better daily, her eyes were less sore and the skin on and around her beak gradually looked more healthy. As she grew more active her true character came to light. She became the ring leader for those swans wanting to avoid treatment and she headed the rush to get into the pond before we could intercept them. Cunningly she would dodge between the trees and then make a dash for the safety of the pond whilst we went the other way. Swans can 'run' quite fast when they need to and how we never fell in the pond I don't know.

Really, this swan tolerated her treatments very well considering she totally resented us being anywhere near her, let alone picking her up and handling her, which seemed to add insult to her injuries.

At this time there were several other swans in care, which, like this swan, had no identification rings. We improvised using loose pieces of bandage tied around one or other leg to help with identification and this was helpful to any staff not well acquainted with them if they needed to go in to give any treatments. One evening someone decided to put a patch of mauve veterinary spray on this particular swan's back; it was quite a good idea as it was harmless to the swan and identified her. Alas! Swans will be swans and in this particular swan's case it meant excessive preening to rid herself of all traces of human contact. This episode resulted in half a white swan at the latter end and, where she had rubbed her head and neck across her back, the front half became a delicate shade of mauve! From then on she was unoriginally named Violet.

As Violet continued to make terrific physical

Shake-down after preening.

progress the same could not be said for her appearance. Her delicate neck feathers began to fall out and the skin on her neck became dry and flaky. Not only was she partially mauve, she was partially bald as well. Poor Violet looked quite ridiculous as she waddled defiantly about the aviary. This didn't bother her at all. She was feeling well and everyone knew it.

Almost three months after being rescued, recovering from lead poisoning, tufts of minute feathers beginning to sprout again on her neck and with barely a tinge of mauve to her name Violet went to join other swans and cygnets for rehabilitation with Steve and Zyllah. She eventually was released back to the wild.

As previously stated I had actually only seen two incidents of oiled swans and I learnt through bitter experience on the first occasion never to attempt their cleaning without training. We simply did not appreciate how specialized a job it is and, although our intentions were honourable, our endeavours were disastrous. A small percentage of the solid tar-like oil was washed off but the swans did not become as clean and waterproof as they were supposed to and the pair were quickly transferred to the special RSPCA centre in Somerset. If only we had known when the swans came in what we later found out. The swans were eventually all right but I am still mortified to this day when I think of our failed attempts.

The effects of oil.

Some years later, after I had left the RSPCA, I saw a pair of swans and their cygnet which had been badly oiled. An attempt had been made to clean them, with disastrous results. They were transferred to a swan sanctuary where the cygnet, suffering from severe hypothermia, died during the night. The pair survived, but in the early stages of their rehabilitation, the male swan became seriously ill and nearly died. He had intensive care for some weeks during which time his mate sat close beside him, and at night could be seen piling bedding material around him to keep him warm, even though they were always taken in from dusk to the next morning. He took some months to recover; the swans moulted, and were eventually released together onto a large, private lake where they have settled happily.

BOAT TRAFFIC/POPULATION ACTIVITY

Heavy boat traffic on popular stretches of our waterways can cause great disturbance to swans and other wildlife. In most instances the various species of wildlife may seem to adapt quite well to changes which the seasons bring; however, concentrated activity of both boats and people does have adverse effects on wildlife and the environment. Particularly in spring and summer, large areas of rivers are frequented by people and boats. The riverbeds are constantly stirred up, which affects the growth of underwater plants; the banks become eroded with the increased flow of water from river traffic, which decreases the ability of natural vegetation to gain a foothold and flourish. This in turn reduces the availability of suitable nesting sites for swans and other waterfowl. The result is a severe decline in the number of areas where swans can live undisturbed and safely breed and where they can find adequate supplies of natural food for themselves and their families. The busiest time on the rivers, ponds and lakes is exactly the time when the swans and other waterfowl require the most privacy and quiet as they begin to build their nests, lay eggs and rear their young.

Although most swans manage to avoid colliding with boat traffic it can be difficult for them to escape injury on very busy waterways, and unfortunately there is a minority of owners of motorboats and speedboats who do not like swans and who deliberately produce accidents. Swans' necks and wings sustain most of the damage from boating accidents, by collision with the actual boat or from oars, and we know that there have been quite a number of these accidents on the

Norfolk Broads as well as some on the Thames and other rivers.

VANDALISM, SHOOTING AND DELIBERATE ACTS OF CRUELTY

Unfortunately for the Mute Swan, it is a large bird and is conspicuous by its brilliant white plumage, so it forms a very slow moving and exceptionally easy target. Swans and cygnets are subjected to many acts of vandalism and deliberate cruelty which are as extensive and varied as the human imagination. Incidents are widespread throughout the country, although in rural areas these possibly aren't publicized. There is a higher percentage in densely populated urban areas: large cities and towns, public parks, ponds and popular stretches of rivers find the swans in far closer proximity to man and in these conditions the swans become more trusting of humans especially where there is a good supply of food. Unfortunately for the swan it usually realizes too late the difference between a human with kind intentions and one that has come to harm it, particularly as the culprits often offer food before they commit their deeds. In many instances there is nothing the swans can do to avoid what befalls them.

I have come across many atrocities and I know that people in other parts of the country see similar things. In such places as the Norfolk Broads, Len Baker has rescued swans purposely hit with oars, or tied up and dragged at speed behind boats, repeatedly run over by bicycles and one swan suffered at the hands of a man who tried to saw its beak off. The birds' injuries include a high percentage of shooting, mostly by airgun pellets but sometimes from shotguns. Injury from airgun pellets is extremely common and many swans and cygnets are admitted into care for this reason but those taken in for treatment for other problems are often found to have been shot as well. Airgun pellets are frequently found whilst handling a bird and a lot are discovered in the process of X–raying the bird for other reasons. The developed radiographs show the presence of airgun pellets, usually the odd one or two, but sometimes a horrifying picture of a mass of pellets. The pellets may be lodged deep in organs or tissues where they are most times impossible to remove without major surgery, and the decision has to be made whether to do this or leave well alone. If the bird is not suffering then the pellets

Injury from airgun pellets: abscess under chin and blindness in one eye.

Airgun pellets.

are usually left; sometimes the tissue forms a 'wall' around the pellet and it causes no problems at all. Where they are obviously not the source of a problem it would be too much to put an already sick bird through. Sometimes we have found pellets lying superficially just under the skin, in wings and legs or in necks and these can often be removed quickly and with a minimum amount of surgical interference, and if it does not stress the swan it is all the better without the pellet.

Pellets can cause considerable swelling and infected wounds. Real problems arise when the swan is shot in the head, which appears to be a favourite target. Quite a lot of swans are shot directly in the eye which obviously results in collapse of the eyeball and blindness. The majority of swans are shot in one eye and they can manage well with the use of the remaining eye, although they are at an obvious disadvantage of

approaching danger on their blind side. Airgun pellets often penetrate quite deeply into the skull and it is impossible to remove these; some swans seem to cope well, though we can't say how much pain they may be in and I have known two swans die as a result of this. Surprisingly, crossbows are another problem: not only domestic pets and ducks on ponds have suffered from them, but also swans. In Norfolk, Len Baker had a particularly devastating case where a swan had been crucified to a tree with three crossbow bolts. It died soon after he rescued it.

Swans are also sometimes shot with shotguns but this seems to occur more in rural areas. The swans may fly in and begin to feed on crops when other food is in short supply. Shot can cause poisoning if it is swallowed.

Often the places where the swans nest are interfered with and even the nests may be destroyed. No matter how carefully local people watch this can still happen, particularly if the nests are easily accessible. Even building a nest on a protected island does not stop the swans from being disturbed as people get onto the islands from boats. They may then steal the eggs; although this act carries a very heavy fine, it does not seem to deter them. Apart from the fact that this practice contributes to the decline of a local population, it causes the parent birds untold distress; even if some eggs are left they may be so upset that they permanently abandon the nest. If they choose to stay, even though they may be physically capable of producing a second clutch of eggs, the stress of disturbance may mean they will not breed again the same year. Dogs are sometimes responsible for attacking swans and we have known instances where an aggressive dog has deliberately been encouraged to attack a swan. As can be seen, the diversity of problems is endless.

During the years I was with the RSPCA I saw a considerable number of incidents which involved deliberate cruelty to swans. I remember one summer's afternoon when the Vintners' swan-marker arrived with the body of a dead female swan. He had been called to the Thames riverside car park at Ham in Surrey by a very distressed man. It had been a beautiful day and the gentleman had decided to go down to the river at lunchtime and feed the birds. An established pair of swans, resident on that stretch of the river, were there and came out of the river and up the slipway to feed by the side of the car park. The pairs of swans were busy feeding when a car full of youths drove into the car park at high speed.

They roared round the area and before the man knew what was happening, the car sped straight towards the swans and hit the female as she was feeding. Within a matter of seconds the car sped off and was gone. In the process of this the female swan had been decapitated and her headless body lay on the ground next to her shocked mate. The man, by now in tears, was also terribly shocked and didn't for a moment know what to do, the car had disappeared so fast that he had no chance to get the registration number, and there he was with a distraught male swan looking at its dead mate. After a minute or two he ran to phone for help. The lone swan went back to the water but after the body was taken away, he continued to patrol his stretch of the river, swimming backwards and forwards calling for his mate for some weeks. Eventually, he moved further down the river towards the non-breeding flock at Hampton, so all we could do was hope that he found company and at a later time another mate.

From my childhood I remember a park keeper in Ewell telling me how one night some boys had climbed the park gates and set fire to the reeds at the edge of the small lake. The swans had their nest there and the flames engulfed the reeds and nest and all the newly hatched cygnets were burnt to death. Years later my suspicions were aroused when I caught sight of three boys hiding behind a bush near a pond. As I watched it seemed that every time the male swan came swimming past the bush the boys did something which made the swan flinch and shake his head. As I walked up behind the boys I saw exactly what they were doing. They had a bag of dried peas and a pea-shooter and as the swan came by they were firing the very hard peas at his eyes. Although this was unlikely to cause him any real harm it obviously stung him; small cruelties like this may lead to worse in the future. The boys clearly looked guilty when I asked them what they were doing but they did not think that there was anything particularly wrong in this! After a lecture they decided to shuffle off, having second thoughts as I offered to try out their pea-shooter on them to find out how much it stung.

Within a few months one year we saw two swans in from London parks: one had been attacked by a dog and the other had been shot. The first call came from park keepers at Burgess Park in London, SE5. The keepers were alerted when members of the public saw a man, in broad daylight, lift his dog (a Rottweiler) over a low fence to attack a female swan. The dog promptly set upon the swan and attacked it before the swan had any chance of escape. The male swan went mad trying to defend his mate. The park keepers rushed to the scene, managed to beat off the dog and arrested the man. They lifted the now limp and terrified female swan to safety. It was decided that it was best to examine the swan to make sure that nothing too serious was wrong. The keepers had wondered whether to keep her quiet somewhere but were afraid she might be badly injured. The swan was examined and no serious injuries were found, only a few grazes. We noticed that she was underweight but at that time she was suffering so badly from shock that she was completely collapsed so she was given all the necessary treatment for this and was left alone in the warm and quiet. She sat as though lifeless, her wings and neck drooping and within a few hours she died. We had hoped that she would make a fairly speedy recovery as we did not want to keep the pair separated.

I had to telephone the park keepers who, already furious over the events, were now clearly most upset. The man involved had already been in trouble some time before for doing the exact same thing. The pair of swans had been together for a long time and they were now anxious as to what could be done for the lone male. There was very little we could do; with time he would be likely to find a new mate but I advised them that

Swan with cygnets.

they watch him closely as long as he stayed within the park, in case he appeared unwell at all. I also gave them some phone numbers of where they might perhaps locate a female that was due for release from rehabilitation, but the choice would be the male swan's, we couldn't choose a mate for him.

The resulting post-mortem of the female swan, carried out at Oxford, was a surprise. It showed that the swan had got lead poisoning and this accounted for her weight loss. No lead weights were found in her gizzard but analysis of samples from body organs and bone showed a high presence of lead. They felt that this had possibly weakened her so she failed to escape from the dog in time and that the stress and lead poisoning combined explained why the swan reacted so badly and died.

Three months after the incident with the swan in Burgess Park we received a phone call from keepers at a park in Dulwich, London. A male swan had happily lived in the park for many years and was the pride and joy of the staff and everyone who knew him. When they went to feed him one morning they noticed that he wasn't as bright as usual and that something seemed to be wrong with his left eye. They brought him into the hospital and at first glance it looked as though

he might have been shot through the eye. They left him with us and I carried him down to be X-rayed.

Apart from his eye he seemed in wonderful condition. I put the swan on the X-ray table and as I looked closely at his head I saw something protruding from the right nostril. With a pair of forceps I got hold of the object and pulled out an airgun pellet. The swan was certainly not very bright and quietly resigned himself to having his head and neck X-rayed in various positions. When the radiographs were developed I saw to my horror that four airgun pellets were embedded in his head, which had penetrated the skull and there was no way they could be removed. (The fifth airgun pellet had done no damage and I had removed that.) The airgun pellet that had blinded him had lodged in his brain. The predicament now for the vets was did we put him to sleep, when he might eventually be all right or did we give him a chance and see what happened, and how much he was suffering at the moment. The eventual decision was to give him what treatment we could, to keep him in the aviary with lots of food and shelter and observe him carefully. I phoned the keepers who were as horrified as I had been; as usual they never saw or heard of anyone shooting birds in their park. They were happy for

On ice.

him to stay and to see what could be done and they rang in daily to find out his progress.

Out in the aviary the swan took some time to adjust but by the end of the day he had eaten well and we settled him down for the night. To begin with he definitely had some bad moments but after the first few days he seemed in good shape. He was in and out of the pond as regularly as the other swans and his appetite was marvellous. Apart from his blind eye he did not now seem at all poorly. The question was whether he would continue to do so well or whether there might be some complications. This question was unfortunately answered on the ninth day he was with us. Without any prior warning he sat down and died. I then had another unpleasant phone call to make. The park keepers were extremely upset; at least, they said, the swan had had a fine life for many years in the park before this happened. I had sent off the swan's BTO ring number and soon received the details. It was surprising to see that this swan had lived to over fifteen years of age. He had originally been ringed in Abingdon, Oxfordshire, as a two year old.

I have only seen one swan that was killed by a shotgun. It was brought in by an inspector. He thought they would be able to bring a prosecution so the swan was X–rayed and a thorough post-mortem was done. The shot had peppered every organ in its body and there was certainly no doubt as to the cause of death. Many of the swans and cygnets with airgun pellets in them of course do manage to survive very well. Steve and Zyllah Cooke had some swans in with enormous swellings under their beaks. These had turned septic after the pellets had entered and because of the difficulty in eating the birds became very unwell. The abscesses were lanced and cleaned and the pellets removed and, given time, the swans recovered.

Fishing hooks, lethal as they can be, are usually picked up by the swans accidentally, but one day we had a swan come in which had been deliberately fed a hook wrapped in a piece of bread. A man had seen children do this and had not been able to act quickly enough before the swan swallowed the bread. The swan was X–rayed but the hook, which was minute, had become embedded in the wall of the oesophagus and the vets couldn't remove it without some pretty drastic surgery. After some days the swan was returned and the warden kept a close watch on him. It was important that if he stopped eating he should come back straight away. Some years later the swan was still on his pond and was fine.

Egg stealing is just downright mean. Cygnet

mortality rate is high anyway and there are areas where swans are lucky if they reach three years of age, and this means that many die before they are old enough to breed.

There was a problem at Ashtead pond two years running as I mentioned before (see p.54). Whoever decided to try and make life difficult for the swans took every single egg the female laid, and the same happened the following year. Both years, when their protective, breeding instincts were at their height, the swans were deprived of their broods. No fox could have got away with stealing six to eight eggs in one night without the parents, particularly the cob, intervening. There were also problems whenever the pond froze over in the winter. Virtually as soon as the ice had formed, we would find that during the night milk bottles would be thrown onto it which of course resulted in the bottles smashing. As the pair of swans, any cygnet or other birds walked across the pond on the ice they could not differentiate between the glistening ice and the colourless jagged glass. We managed to remove the glass safely before any of the birds were severely injured.

In 1983 gravel pits near the M4 motorway needed to be drained and filled in when the M25/M4 interchange began to be built. A group of swans that had been living there had flown away but one swan remained and refused to leave. (This is not an experience of mine, but a much abbreviated version which tells of the many, many hours that Tim Heron spent helping to rescue and constantly trying to protect a very beautiful and much loved swan.)

The lone swan had been there for several months and was causing considerable concern to passing motorists. They duly phoned and reported their concern. At that time 'Save Our Swans' was in operation and Tim went out, as did the RSPCA, on numerous rescue attempts but the swan continued to elude capture. Costains Cementation who were constructing the interchange were also concerned for the swan and assisted in any way they could. Attempts continued and one evening in July, after much crafty manoeuvring, Tim and his fellow rescuers finally caught the wily swan. By this time the swan had become known as the Artful Dodger.

The feathers on Dodger's underside had become worn away and a large callus had formed on his breastbone. Much of the ground had become baked by the hot summer sun and had cracked into deep fissures. They suspected that the swan had worn away the skin on his breastbone by

The Artful Dodger evades capture.

hauling himself over the steep rough ground.

Later, in the following January when the callus had healed, Dodger was released to join the swans at Dinton Pastures beyond Reading in Berkshire. During March he disappeared and a few days later came reports of sightings of a lone swan newly arrived on a small village pond a mile or so away. There was some concern at this because it was feared that the swan would be in trouble if it tried to fly out from such a small area. There had been reports that at least one swan had been killed by hitting power cables near the pond whilst trying to fly out.

On checking the pond, Tim found that sure enough it was his old friend the Dodger and it was

decided to remove him for his own safety. Tim said that the Dodger looked at him with a wary glint in his eye but as he was a fairly greedy bird his stomach got the better of him and he approached for food. With barely a ruffled feather Tim picked up the Dodger and transported him back to Dinton.

Within a week the swan had disappeared again and when Tim went to check, there was Dodger back on his chosen pond, which was where he obviously wanted to stay. People also worried because at times this bold swan had seemed far too close to the road for his own safety, but they knew they couldn't make the swan live some-

The Artful Dodger is captured.

where he didn't want to, so he would just have to take his chances. A few months later, someone reported seeing blood on Dodger so he was rescued and examined. It appeared he had strained one of his legs and after some minor treatment in care he was taken back to his pond. He lived there until, in 1986, someone shot him with a .22 airgun pellet and the Artful Dodger was dead.

REFUSE

Just about everywhere we go it appears we are accompanied by a singularly unpleasant, recurrent problem – litter. As soon as a place is tidied up it all appears again, day after day, month after month, year after year. Much of what is deliberately discarded is not bio-degradable and is therefore accumulative. With the provision of council household refuse collections, local rubbish dumps and litter bins, the situation gets worse instead of better.

Apart from the fact that all this rubbish is revolting to look at, and frequently smelly, it is often very dangerous, not only to adults, children and domestic pets but to wildlife. Items such as broken glass, bottles, tin cans and food wrappers are particularly lethal as birds and animals are attracted by the smell of these and can become badly injured from sharp edges, may get their heads stuck or, if small enough, often enter the container and become trapped inside, left to suffer a slow death unless found. We all know of people whose dogs receive cut feet whilst out walking and that most times they need some form of treatment. What happens to free-roaming wild animals and birds that suffer the same injuries?

Whenever my friends and I are out checking on swans we always see litter and whenever possible we try to collect what we can and dispose of it. It is a depressing sight to see all the water birds wading through floating debris at the slipways and riverbanks. I could never have imagined what rubbish lies below the water level of a river, until one day I joined an organized river clearance at Richmond-upon-Thames. The locks had been closed at Hampton and the water level dropped considerably to enable us to retrieve as much as possible from a wide area of the river margins. The council had supplied large skips which became full very quickly. We collected many sacks of rubbish, fishing tackle and food wrappers amongst the smaller items. A little way along the riverbed at a slipway close to a pub we found loads of beer mugs and wine glasses, some of which were broken. The summer months were far worse for this problem where crowds of people stood out by the river during the fine evenings. Great chunks of twisted sharp pieces of metal were also pulled up and removed, parts of cars, bicycles, water tanks and metal pipes had been deposited here. I then fully realized what obstacles all the water birds have to contend with living on the rivers.

Kingston-upon-Thames was almost as bad and one well known chain store must have been very short of their shopping trolleys. This was just a small portion of the riverside that I had seen in this state and I wondered what percentage of other rivers are like this.

The pond at Ashtead suffered from the same problem, despite a local group's efforts weekly to keep the place clean and tidy and the provision of new litter bins by the Mole Valley Council. Much litter accumulated within the fenced area around the swans' nest. The direction that the winter winds blew in brought litter across the pond to this particular corner and once the swans began nesting again it was of course impossible to go anywhere near this part of the pond. Every spring the female swan could be seen incubating her eggs surrounded on her nest by a selection of litter, and this was the environment the cygnets had to hatch out into.

I remember the Vintners' swanmarker telling me of a cygnet he was called to rescue some years ago. A metal ring-pull tab from a tin can had become caught around the cygnet's tongue and part of its beak. It was fortunate that it was removed in time as, not only could the cygnet not feed, but it would have eventually suffered a terrible injury.

At Walton-on-the-Hill in Surrey I was called to check on a large male swan at a pond. A lady had seen a length of green plastic trailing under the swan. I watched for a long time but could see nothing. The cob was not very amenable and would not approach for food, his mate was on the nest incubating and he was in full protective mood. The next day I went back, the plastic had been seen again, and it was obvious he had to be caught and examined. Luckily this time the cob was resting on a grassy bank of the pond by the edge of someone's garden. They let me through their house and I climbed over the low fence onto the grass. The cob was immediately awake and standing, a few pieces of bread stopped his retreat to the pond and I managed to catch him with the swan-hook just as he reached the water. After

Adult resting.

being used to dealing with many underweight swans this cob came as a shock. He was very, very strong and about the heaviest swan I'd ever handled.

With his powerful wings under control and with him restrained as I knelt over him with my legs on either side of his body, I finally saw the green plastic line. A piece of green garden netting, the type used for growing runner beans, had become caught round his neck. As the holes on this netting were large his neck was through one hole and it had stretched under his body and one leg was caught through another hole.

The lady in the house gave me a pair of scissors to cut the plastic and the swan was soon free. Except for the tiny piece of plastic trailing by his leg the rest had become invisible beneath his feathers. As I stood up the swan made a very hasty escape to the pond. The netting only measured about four inches by six inches but stretched considerably and could have been lethal.

8 Release

After the often lengthy and sometimes complicated process of helping a swan back to perfect health comes yet another problem, that of release. This can be just as much a cause for concern as the original stages of nursing. By the very nature of the work, the long hours spent in observing and treating the swans and cygnets, we often become over-protective of them. Ultimately they will decide where they are going to live. Anyone who has ever been involved with the care of swans knows only too well what a worry the release of swans and cygnets can be and the sense of responsibility that this places on those concerned. We have no choice but to release these birds back into an environment where injury and illness are highly likely to occur again. This is why there is always an effort made to find places that are known to be safer than the so-called 'high risk' areas, places such as private lakes, and areas which are not highly populated, or known to be the territory of dominant pairs of swans. There the swans and cygnets may have the best chance possible to begin a free life again. If they choose to fly out to other areas we have no control over this but in their first stages of release the least we can do is not to return them immediately to an area where they are doomed.

A percentage of all recovered birds at some time come into care again and it is sad that some of these birds die as a result of hazards they have encountered when released. There is no such finer moment than when one sees a swan released. To see the excitement in the swan as it views the open space of water, the first rush to freedom, the point at which it spreads its wings and takes off across the water and then to watch as it splashes with joy and preens. It is also a sad moment, hoping that it will fare safely in the future, whether it will return into care again but ultimately remembering the day it arrived as a former shadow of itself, often with no will to live. At that precise moment everyone involved knows that all the intensive care was worth every second it took.

9 Natural Hazards

Natural causes of death are wide ranging and include such problems as enteritis, pneumonia, avian tuberculosis, internal parasitic infestations, congenital defects (in which case tiny cygnets may be killed or abandoned by their parents), botulism (caused by a toxic organism, seen chiefly in hot, dry prolonged spells of weather), old age and its associated problems of organ dysfunction, flying accidents, starvation in harsh winter months and predation by dogs and foxes, with young cygnets possible predation by pike also, and territorial fights.

BOTULISM

Botulism, a naturally occurring organism, produces poisonous toxins in certain conditions of stagnant water. All water birds can be exposed to this danger. Botulism is commonly seen in swans and other waterfowl when there has been a prolonged spell of hot weather with little or no rainfall, but may also occur at other times of the

year. The water level drops and the water becomes stagnant; vegetation and silt get stirred up. The organism multiplies and the resulting toxin can be swallowed by birds. I only saw a few cases of botulism when I was at 'Save Our Swans' in Windsor but Steve and Zyllah Cooke had dealt with many cases over several consecutive summers.

The organism responsible is called *Clostridium botulinum*. Although there are various types it is usually Type C which is present. There is often little that can be done for water birds suffering from this except to remove them from the area and to take them into care. Birds affected with this illness become extremely sick very quickly and often die before anything can be done to help them. Swans become completely paralysed, and show signs of respiratory distress, are therefore unable to swim, walk or stand and can be seen sitting with their necks and wings outstretched on the ground.

One year in August, the Vintners' swanmarker

brought an adult female swan into us at Putney. The swan was extremely sick and in fact died shortly after she arrived. The female swan had had the classic symptoms of botulism though she had been in very good bodily condition a short time before.

INFECTIONS AND PARASITES

Swans are prone to various infections such as enteritis, pneumonia, aspergillosis and avian tuberculosis.

I have seen enteritis in quite a few swans which otherwise seemed in good physical condition. As advised, a short course of antibiotics had seen them return to good health. Pneumonia is sometimes seen in swans and cygnets suffering from hypothermia and sometimes as a result of oiling. Cygnets are often admitted suffering either from septicaemia or a fever of unknown origin for which suitable antibiotics form the basis of therapy.

Aspergillosis is a fungal infection caused by the inhalation of spores of *Aspergillus fumigatus*, which are present in straw, hay and some grains. Symptoms include gaping, difficulty in breathing and a wheezy cough, and it is very hard to cure. We were always worried about the use of straw for bedding but there was little else available that provided the necessary warmth and support for recumbent swans suffering from hypothermia.

In 1982 we had a dead swan brought into the hospital from Wimbledon Park which went to Oxford for post-mortem. This showed that the swan had lead poisoning as well as avian tuberculosis but due to the extensive damage to the organs from both illnesses it was not possible to say which had been the ultimate cause of death.

Swans also have internal parasites such as heartworms and roundworms but it is often difficult to determine if these are the actual cause of an illness. Roundworms and tapeworms are common in cygnets and treatment is given when this is evident although even quite a high presence of these worms appears generally to cause little debilitation. One dead swan was post-mortemed from Lancashire which had a heavy infestation of worms related to roundworms. The general opinion was that these had been contracted by the swan eating small crustaceans which were the intermediate host of this particular worm. Occasionally where symptoms of any routine illness we were used to were not obvious, we were advised to worm swans with a broad-spectrum wormer in case of intestinal worm infestation.

Swans also have external parasites – not the

most pleasant of creatures, namely large and exceedingly mobile biting lice. Although host specific and not living on humans they are not averse to a quick scuttle about one's person. My first encounter with these was one of total horror. An extremely debilitated collapsed swan was brought in with lead poisoning one day and it appeared that lice leave their host when sick like rats leaving a sinking ship. Suddenly I was covered in these large, adult dark brown lice which as soon as I saw them disappeared into my clothing. The next stage was a feeling of 'things' moving that could not be located and then I felt them on my scalp. They move so fast that they are very difficult to catch. Generally they tend to stay on the swan and then when disturbed scramble out of sight deeper into the swan's feathers. They are feather lice which feed on debris from the skin and feathers of their host. With a very sick swan the lice often multiply considerably which results in irritation and poor condition of the feathers. In the nymphal stage they are white and much smaller and are not as easily detected if they leave their host, so a good investigation of one's clothing afterwards does much for one's peace of mind! Eventually I became used to them but it could be embarrassing to watch someone else's expression change as they suddenly saw an unsavoury-looking bug appear out of the collar of my uniform and scuttle up my neck only to disappear into my hair. They're even more disgusted when you say 'it's only lice'.

CONGENITAL ABNORMALITIES

Congenital abnormalities include such problems as deformities of the beak. Some swans' beaks develop so that the lower mandible extends beyond a shorter upper mandible and, depending on severity, because it causes considerable difficulty in eating, may lead to the swan dying of starvation; however some swans are known to survive well with such a deformity.

Deformities of the wing sometimes occur and the so-called 'airplane wing' may be seen in swans, where the tips of their wings appear to stick out at right angles. This is caused by rotation of the carpal joint (wrist) which projects outwards. Swans with such wing deformities are unable to fly and are usually released to the safer places such as private lakes.

In 1984 Zyllah Cooke was called to rescue a male swan which had mysteriously appeared in an alleyway behind the Wimpy Bar in West Drayton, Middlesex. The swan turned out to be in perfect health except that he had a deformed beak. The upper mandible was shorter than the lower mandible, and, although this caused him some difficulty in eating, he managed well. Since

the time of his first release with a female swan to a private lake 'Wimpy' has had many adventures. In the beginning he got himself into trouble by harassing horses in a neighbouring field and had to be relocated with his companion. But within a few days 'Wimpy' took off and then had to be rescued from the River Kennet at Reading as he had landed in the territory of a resident pair of swans which attacked him.

In the spring of 1986 he was released with a different female swan to another safe sheltered lake where he could be observed. During their summer moult they went for a long walk and were found exhausted in someone's garden. They were taken back whilst their moult continued and with new flight feathers grown the female took off. 'Wimpy' was obviously lonely because he flew back to the rehabilitation centre.

Seemingly able to fend for himself, needing freedom and the company of other swans he was released to join the flock at Windsor and here he stayed apart from the odd short sortie to and fro. His second female companion appeared at Windsor the following winter and they were reunited. They remained quite close and it was hoped that they would eventually establish a territory together. Tragedy occurred when Wimpy's friend was killed in May 1987 when she flew into Slough

Wimpy's deformed beak.

Sewage Works.

'Wimpy' maintains a home base with the rest of the flock at Windsor and is a frequent visitor to the little café by the Promenade. He has proved to be a swan as individual in his character as he is in his appearance. He remains a firm favourite with everyone that knows him and by some very beguiling tactics he has managed to acquire many advantages due to his deformity which gives him a very appealing expression.

FLYING ACCIDENTS – CRASHLANDINGS

Flying accidents occur for many reasons; although the injuries sustained from these accidents may be minor or severe, death frequently results. From the air things can look very deceptive for a swan: there are numerous obstacles for large birds such as swans to avoid. They frequently fly into pylons and power cables. Cables are very difficult for the swans to see and usually have lethal consequences, the 'lucky' ones that survive this hazard are often badly burned or suffer horrendous wing injuries. Other factors such as poor visibility in bad weather conditions considerably increase the risk of accidents. From the

Crashlanded swan.

air, wet roads and motorways resemble open expanses of water, particularly when the sun is out and shimmers on the tarmac. The impact of landing on this is immense and swans are often killed as they hit roads, but those that withstand the landing can have severe and permanently disabling injuries such as badly broken wings and legs. Wings sometimes have to be amputated if repair of the fracture is impossible, and as the swans' flying days come to an end a place needs to be found, if they eventually recover, where they can live the rest of their days in relative safety. Areas such as private lakes are often sought out and these days there are many people who are delighted to have such birds on their property. Those swans and cygnets that receive only mild injuries are in the minority and usually suffer quite severe bruising, particularly to the chest and abdomen, along with various cuts and grazes. These birds are generally kept under observation for some time as there is always the likelihood of internal haemorrhage and complications. With crashlandings on roads there is the added danger to both bird and man of collisions with oncoming traffic.

Any of these birds which are unwell when they take to the air are at great risk from accidents as they may become exhausted more quickly and their judgment is impaired. Illnesses such as lead poisoning are known to affect their overall awareness and cause disorientation. Obviously those that are very ill are unlikely to fly at all.

Fledgling cygnets and juvenile swans are particularly prone to accidents. As inexperienced fliers they may have only flown short distances previously or may even be on a maiden flight; coupled with this a poor knowledge of the surrounding area puts them at greater risk. Swans do also fly into buildings and bridges; a last minute decision to alter course, for whatever reason, is often too late for this heavy bird and not easily within its manoeuvring capabilities.

I have seen swans brought in which have died on impact when they have crashlanded, and also ones which have unfortunately died shortly after being rescued and brought in for treatment, but others have been luckier, made complete recoveries and eventually been released.

I well remember a cygnet which was brought in by an inspector who had been called to rescue the bird off the M4 motorway. As the cygnet was almost fully grown but still had very mottled feathers we assumed that it probably had little flying experience. It was a fine day and the bird was in perfect health so it could even have been on a maiden flight. The cygnet was extremely lucky to have sustained only minor injuries; not only had it survived the hard impact of its untimely landing but it had not come into contact with any vehicles either. The cygnet was obviously very shocked and when it had recovered a little it was thoroughly examined. There were no broken bones, and, although severely bruised, apart from minor cuts and grazes on its neck and the joints of its legs and wings, the most serious injury seemed to be muscle strain of one wing. It was important to watch the cygnet carefully during its first few days in care to make sure that no complictions arose from any possible internal damage. The minor cuts were stitched and the now useless wing needed support so it was positioned in its resting state close to the body and held in place with Elastoplast. The plaster had to be attached around the bird's body, over the injured wing and under the good wing which it was left free to move. After all this was over, we had a safe but singularly unimpressed cygnet. The next few hours were spent meticulously attempting to unpick the strapping but it finally gave up and decided to have some food. Having more or less resigned itself to its predicament, the next necessary thing to do was to have a good swim, which it wasn't allowed to (because the plaster had to remain dry). This caused no end of frustration for the poor cygnet. It had been placed in a run near the swans in the aviary with the thought that the sight of others of its kind would help to settle it, but the sight of the pond full of lovely clean water with swans swimming in it meant the cygnet pressed its beak to the wire mesh and tried to push its way through.

This was almost as frustrating for us to watch as it was for the cygnet so we moved it to a run further out of sight where it preened what ruffled feathers it could get at. More frustration was yet to come for the cygnet, because as we hosed down the exercise runs and the concrete several times a day I could almost see its eyes light up. Water and lots of it! Finally, I took to hosing it with a very light spray a couple of times a day and this it thoroughly enjoyed; without the Elastoplast support getting soaked the cygnet was able to have a shower; it brightened up considerably and became more particular about its preening.

After two weeks the stitches were removed from its now healed wounds and at three weeks came the testing date for its wing. Slowly we removed the sticky plaster from around its body, a slow process because the feathers had stuck very firmly to it. To begin with the cygnet stood quietly gazing round at us, the wing still slightly drooping. We had expected this as it hadn't been used but hoped after an hour or so of use it would look better. (It was clearly a momentous occasion for the cygnet.) Suddenly, both wings started to twitch, then to kind of shuffle, speed was gathered and then frantic flapping of both wings began as the cygnet raised its head with outstretched neck and snorted approval. I picked the cygnet up and carried it to the aviary. It could hardly reach the pond fast enough and the next hour passed with the cygnet going berserk, rolling, splashing and flapping its wings in the water whilst the rest of the swans cleared off to a safer distance and stood and watched. Later on, the cygnet was tucking into the food, with both wings held firmly in the right position. It stayed with us a while longer to gain strength and it was then released to a non-breeding flock where we thought it might stay, hopefully a wiser bird.

During the winter of 1987 I was called to rescue a cygnet from someone's back garden near Carshalton in Surrey. There had been a continuous heavy snowfall and it was so bitterly cold that all the ponds, smaller lakes and parts of rivers had frozen over. The almost fully grown cygnet had probably decided to look for alternative accommodation, must have taken to the air and then discovered that everything around it looked the same.

The owner of the property decided to clear the footpaths at the back of the house that morning and was astounded, as he rounded the corner of the house, to see huge footprints in the snow. As he turned to look around further he was confronted by an equally surprised, enormous mottled bird which stood up and began to emit threatening hissing noises. The gentleman speedily retired to the safety of his kitchen where he spied upon the bird and began to deliberate his course of action. Why do things always happen at a weekend? he thought. He spent all of the morning and most of the afternoon trying to track someone down who could come out and relieve him of his visitor but he phoned every available authority he could think of to no avail. Everyone was on emergency duty, weighed under with real life-and-death calls, the difficult weather conditions meant that it was taking twice as long as usual to travel anywhere. Finally, through a friend and a trail of various RSPB members, he phoned 'Swan Lifeline'. I was then phoned as I was the nearest person they knew of. By this time it was five o'clock and dark. I was certainly able to get the cygnet but my car was still snowed in. The drifts had been so deep and continuous that I decided it was less trouble to walk to work and forget about the car for the time being, and now I

needed it! This problem was soon solved as the family very kindly said they would come out and collect me from work. On reaching their house I crept out into the garden and there was the cygnet, obviously safe and well but standing gingerly on top of a four-foot snow drift. Its wide webbed feet were doing a splendid job of keeping it from sinking but I knew I would not be as lucky, so after as devious and nonchalant an approach as I could manage I grabbed the suspicious cygnet before we sank into the snow. Within a few minutes I was back in the kitchen and we prepared for our return journey, a large plastic carrier bag being placed over the cygnet's nether regions. Back at the vet's where I worked the cygnet was thoroughly examined and was one hundred per cent fit and well. After its cushioned landing in the snowdrifts of Carshalton the only thing it required was plenty of food as it was by now very hungry. Having set up a large kennel for it and a substantial supply of food and water I left it to settle in and feed for a while before finally checking all was well and turning out the lights.

We had decided that as the cygnet was at the age where it was no longer dependent on its

Juvenile swans and cygnets from a non-breeding flock.

parents the safest place for it was to join the non-breeding flock at Windsor. The morning dawned and after an hour spent digging my car out I set off to collect the cygnet. The cygnet was fine and raring to go, and on the journey to Windsor it looked eagerly out of the car windows. On reaching the promenade at Windsor I carried the cygnet to where the flock were feeding. I placed it on the ground beside the water's edge and stood back thinking there would be a frantic struggle to be quickly released but it stood there and stared, as if in disbelief, at the other forty odd swans and cygnets suddenly before it. I gave the cygnet a gentle push on its tail feathers and it slipped slowly into the water, amongst the crowd of others eagerly waiting to be fed. After a few harmless pecks it was accepted into the group and after a bit of a preen it began to feed. I stayed to watch for a while but all was well and so I left the cygnet to its new life.

A few days later it was ringed by the zoologists from Oxford with a darvic ring and as the cygnet matured it turned out that 'it' is a 'he'. He has since remained with the flock and it was nice to be able to tell the family that their surprise visitor had met with a happy ending and that they will be able to identify him if they ever visit Windsor before he matures and flies away.

In 1988 he hit a bridge and crashlanded again but after a time in care he recovered and was released back to the river.

DEATH OF A MATE

Once paired most swans stay together throughout their lives but if a mate dies or a pair fails to breed then the swans will usually look for a new mate. The younger swans often find a replacement mate quite quickly whilst older, more established birds may take time to adjust. No one can tell whether a swan may die from a 'broken heart'; most of us probably like to believe it is possible but this would generally be dismissed as sentimentality. However I heard of a swan which lost its mate and this perfectly healthy swan completely changed in its behaviour and within two weeks was also dead. Swans certainly pine, as was the case in the bereaved swan at Ham. In a situation where a pair are raising cygnets and one of the parents dies the remaining swan continues to rear the family by itself. Most swans seem to adapt well given time and from watching various single swans it would appear to be beneficial to the widowed swan to be preoccupied with raising a

Loss of a mate.

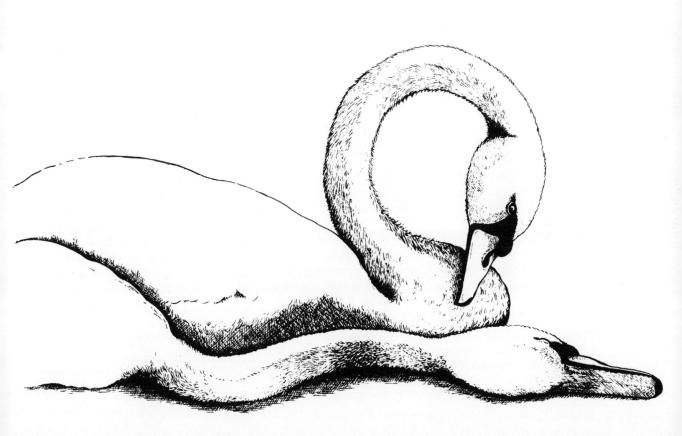

family when such a tragedy occurs.

One February afternoon saw the arrival of a pair of swans from a South London park. The keepers had been concerned that their swans were beginning to show signs of illness and the male swan collapsed a short time later. The inspector who collected them radioed in a message whilst on his way to the hospital to say that both were ill but that the male was in a very bad way. I expected the worst and that was, indeed, what I saw. As soon as they arrived both swans went through the usual preliminary weighing and blood sampling and were then X–rayed. The radiographs showed very small particles of lead in their gizzards but no lead had apparently been recently swallowed; it therefore looked as though both swans had been progressively ill for quite some time before there were any outward signs. The female had also been shot in her right thigh but this was causing no immediate problems; we would think about that later, at that time she had more pressing needs to attend to. Both the swans were underweight, particularly the male who felt very bony wherever we touched him. The female was more difficult to assess. She was quite the tiniest swan I had ever seen and weighed in at eleven pounds but I had no idea what she should have normally weighed. Because she was white, so tiny and as it was February she was duly named 'Snowdrop'.

Snowdrop was obviously very ill but, although quiet and depressed, she was able to walk and stand and thankfully had not reached the same dramatic stage as that of her mate. He, on the other hand, had just about everything wrong that was possible. Plus his severe weight loss he was so ill he couldn't move, his pulse was terribly weak and hardly evident whilst his heartbeat was erratic. He was also dehydrated, his eyeballs moved uncontrollably backwards and forwards and his head was becoming swollen with fluid. We doubted that anything would save him but he was given emergency treatment and a chance to see if any slight improvement would give us hope. We made him as comfortable as possible whilst I began Snowdrop's treatment. I also tube-fed her and then left the two swans together in peace. I constantly kept a close watch on them but after several hours the male swan was totally collapsed and virtually comatose and it was very clear that he would not survive. After some discussion I informed the park keepers of the situation and we put the swan to sleep.

I was by now extremely worried what effect this would have on Snowdrop; the sudden departure of her mate could increase stress and cause her to give up the struggle against her illness. It was therefore very important that she had the company of other swans and, weather permitting, I put her out with the others recovering in the aviary for as long as possible each day. As her treatment and feeds continued she began to pick up and by the fifth day had started to eat. She appeared to be suffering no ill from the loss of her mate and soon latched onto another swan, an adult male, which she followed everywhere.

As the days passed, Snowdrop and her new 'friend' made steady progress. They both would be in care for some months as he also had been very ill and neither of them were off the critical list yet. With an increasing number of new arrivals the aviary began bulging at the seams so Snowdrop and company were transferred to Windsor to continue treatment and rehabilitation there. She slowly but steadily improved but the particular swan she liked took a turn for the worse and did not recover. Once again she was a lone female, but the bond had not been so strong as to present problems and within a short time she formed a strong attachment to yet another swan. As some months passed, their rehabilitation came to an end and the day dawned when they were both fit enough to be released so they were ringed and went together to the freedom of a private lake.

10 Ways to Help

There are many practical ways in which people can help the swans. Regular checkings of local swans and keen observation of swans in general wherever one is can help enormously to safeguard them from the many hazards they face. Any swans or cygnets seen in distress, whether injured or suspected to be generally unwell can be reported to the nearest available authority. This may be a nearby local lock keeper who will be able to phone for help; on the Thames this may be an official swanmarker, or it may be the local RSPCA Inspector in this and other areas, or a special swan charity. These charities have the backup of professional advice and expert help of veterinary surgeons.

An incident reported should state, where possible, any identifying ring numbers, the actual time and location, and what the problem appears to be. It is helpful if someone can maintain observation of the bird until help arrives (a few contact numbers are listed on p.123). It is never advisable to attempt to rescue or handle a swan oneself as not only may this lead to further injury for the bird but also to you.

During the winter extra food supplies to swans and cygnets will make an enormous difference to their health and ability to survive.

If you own a pond or lake suitable for swans and would like to offer a home, the charities are always interested to know.

Equally important, but at all times of the year, is the collection and safe disposal of any items of refuse or fishing tackle wherever they are seen. It is easy to make a valuable contribution by doing this on one's own or some people prefer to be more actively involved by joining a local conservation group which may organize special clearances.

It is also important to help educate family and friends, particularly youngsters, and to point out the problems they may inadvertently cause when fishing. Encouraging youngsters to join a local angling club is a good idea as not only do they get help and support with their pastime, but they are taught to follow the Anglers Code of Conduct which the official clubs uphold.

Last but not least, the swan charities are always in need of help with fundraising or sometimes with contacts for surplus foodstuffs such as bread and greens. For these swan charities, which care day and night for sick and injured swans, fund-raising forms a vital part of the charities' ability to survive and continue with their demanding and important work. Such things as coffee mornings, cheese and wine parties or barbecues amongst friends can help raise a substantial amount of money and everyone enjoys themselves and makes a generous contribution to the suffering swans and cygnets at the same time.

In whatever way we choose to become involved, whether a long- or a short-term commitment, every bit of help is invaluable and every effort is worthwhile.

Contact Telephone Numbers for Swan Rescue, Treatment and Rehabilitation

Swan Lifeline
Covers the Thames Valley and South-East England
Telephone: Slough 75894

Swan Rescue Europe
Based at Shotesham St Mary, Norfolk
Telephone: 0508 42248/428357

Egham Swan Sanctuary
Based at Egham, Surrey
Telephone: Staines 63213

RSPCA
For local Inspectors, phone nearest Central Control listed in local telephone directory.

Thames Water Authorities
Supply telephone numbers of Queen's swankeeper and Vintners' and Dyers' swanmarkers for swans on the River Thames.

Addresses for printed information
(There is usually a charge for fact sheets)

The Department of the Environment
2 Marsham Street, London, SW1P 3EB
(For legislation details)

RSPCA Headquarters
(Wildlife Department), The Causeway, Horsham, West Sussex RH12 1HG

RSPB
The Lodge, Sandy, Bedfordshire SG19 2DL

British Trust for Ornithology
Beech Grove, Tring, Hertfordshire HP23 5NR

Records details of ringed birds found dead, injured or taken into care.
(The trust exists to encourage and promote research by amateurs.)

Reports of swans sighted with darvic rings should be sent to:
Mr Carl Mitchell
The Wildfowl Trust
Slimbridge
Glos GL2 7BT
from where they will be forwarded to the ringer. Reports should give ring colour, number, letter sequence, right or left leg, place and date of sighting and any additional useful information, e.g. whether paired, nesting, with cygnets, etc. The flocks at Windsor, Reading and Hampton are well recorded.

Further Reading

First Aid and Care of Wild Birds by J.E. Cooper and J.T. Eley (David and Charles, 1979)
Swans of the World by Sylvia Bruce Wilmore (out of print) (Taplinger)
Egg – Nature's Miracle of Packaging by Robert Burton (Collins, 1987)
The Mute Swan by Mike Birkhead and Chris Perrins (Croom Helm, 1986)
Birds, Their Structure and Function by A.S. King and J. McLelland (Bailliere Tindall, 1984)
Avian Medicine and Surgery by B.H. Coles (Blackwell Scientific Publications, 1985)
First Aid and Care of Wildlife by Richard Mark Martin (David and Charles, 1984)
Lead Poisoning in Swans (working group report of 1981: Nature Conservancy Council)
White Spirit, Fly Free by Pamela Townsend (Corgi, 1984) (about Len and Sheila Baker of 'Swan Rescue Europe', in Norfolk)
Anglers' Choice: a guide to alternatives to lead weights. (Produced by the RSPB in conjunction with the National Federation of Anglers)
RSPB Information: fact sheet on lead poisoning in swans and non-toxic substitutes
Details of the Control of Pollution Act (Anglers' Lead Weights) Regulations 1986 available from the Department of the Environment